Teaching Young Writers to
Elaborate

Megan S. Sloan

NEW YORK • TORONTO • LONDON • AUCKLAND • SYDNEY
MEXICO CITY • NEW DELHI • HONG KONG • BUENOS AIRES

Teaching Resources

Dedicated to
Jean and George Sullivan,
my parents and first teachers.

To Katie and Julia—my sunshine.

Cover design by Brian LaRossa
Cover photograph by Jason R. Alley
Interior design by Melinda Belter
Interior photographs courtesy of the author
Acquiring and development editor: Gloria Pipkin
ISBN-13 978-0-545-03298-8
ISBN-10 0-545-03298-9
Copyright © 2008 by Megan S. Sloan

2 3 4 5 6 7 8 9 10   40   14 13 12 11 10 09 08

TABLE OF CONTENTS

ACKNOWLEDGMENTS

Many people supported me during this process and I would like to thank them.

First, to the many students who allowed their work to be shared in this book, I thank you.

To Bonnie Campbell Hill and Nancy Johnson for your encouragement and valuable feedback during this process.

To Sam Sebesta, who first taught me to write for publication. You inspire me!

To Brenda Wolf for sharing your students' work and being a good friend.

To Barb Wagner for introducing me to Flip's Fantastic Journal.

To Cyndi Giorgis, Katherine Schlick-Noe, Toni Munizza, Corrine Brandvold, Melissa Burns, Carrie Davison, Stephanie Campbell, Theresa McGrath, Jenny Halstead, Stephanie Hanson, and Kary Thome—thank you for your friendship and support.

To Julie Filer for helping to create very useful assessment forms (particularly the one in this book) and for being a wonderful colleague and friend.

To Connie Roepke for sharing writing ideas for the last 23 years. You have taught me much and have been a dear friend, too.

To Cynthia Heffernan for allowing me to share your experience. You are an exemplary teacher and friend.

To all the teachers, students, and parents at Cathcart Elementary School.

To my editor, Gloria Pipkin—You are incredibly wise. Your guidance and support have been invaluable. I thank you for sharing my vision. I consider you my friend.

To Virginia Dooley for making this into a beautiful book. Thank you.

To my family (especially my sister Nora), friends, and husband, Frank. Thank you for your love and support throughout this project and always.

*I*NTRODUCTION

When I began teaching, twenty years ago, I walked into the classroom without any clear guidance about how to teach writing to young children. I figured that somehow I had missed a crucial day in my teacher education classes— the one where the instructor actually taught us how to teach writing. I honestly don't remember anyone even mentioning the topic.

It wasn't until my first year teaching that I took a class on the writing process. It helped me to see that writers don't just sit down and write; they plan, think, revise, edit, and do it all over again. I began reading and studying the experts of the time: Lucy Calkins, Donald Graves, and Donald Murray, to name a few. I learned that good writing is about voice, elaborating on ideas, writing for a purpose, using specific language, grabbing one's readers with a lead, leaving them satisfied with a conclusion, and more.

I began reviewing the books I liked, asking myself why I liked them. Why was I connecting with these texts? Did I love the language? Did the author describe the settings in ways to make me feel as though I were there? How did the author tell more?

Beginning With Students

In my classroom, I decided to start with what made sense to me. I began by showing students that writers write for different purposes and different audiences. We explored the reasons why we write: to tell our stories, to entertain, to give information, to convey messages such as "thank you" or "get well." We also explored our audiences: teachers, family members, friends, other students, and ourselves.

I began teaching them how we get ideas using different strategies: drawing, talking, or having an experience. And I taught students about drafting, revising, and editing— modeling all of these with my own writing. As students practiced they became more independent, writing for longer periods of time with every workshop.

At this point, I knew I needed to add lessons focused on the content of the writing. So I began to think about ways I could model and conduct lessons in which I taught students about choosing topics, adding details, using rich language, and starting their pieces with sentences that grabbed the reader. I also taught about using the letters that make the sounds in words, and about spacing, capital letters, and punctuation.

Today, I know that I need to observe students, looking for their areas of strength and their areas of need. I plan my lessons to fit these. For instance, if I have a group of first graders who are drawing pictures and are able to write one sentence to match their pictures, I may focus a few lessons on adding details. If my second graders are jumping right into their writing, forgetting to set the reader up with clear first sentences, I might focus on leads.

The Focus of This Book

To teach my students writing, I know I need to teach about finding ideas, organizing text, connecting to a reader, writing with appropriate voice and style, choosing specific and interesting language, and using correct conventions. In a good piece of writing, all of these elements are woven together. However, teachers often focus on just one or two elements in a lesson to highlight their importance. That is what I am doing in this book. I include lessons that highlight the importance of choosing an appropriate topic and elaborating on ideas. There is so much to learn and teach about how writers choose a writing topic to write about, and about how they add details to make that topic live and breathe.

However, I never cease to be amazed at the power of intentional teaching. Knowing your objective and teaching with purpose will result in great learning. Scaffolding with modeled and shared writing experiences will give students the support they need. And time to write will provide students with opportunities for practice. I hope this book helps you discover some new ways to teach students about choosing topics and elaborating on ideas. Take these ideas, tweak them to fit the needs of your students, and make them your own.

A FRAMEWORK FOR TEACHING WRITING

"I don't know what to write about."

"I can't think of anything else to add."

"My brain is empty. There is nothing else important in my story."

We have all heard comments like these from our students on occasion (maybe more often than we would like to admit). Students often struggle with choosing a topic. Elaborating on an idea can be equally difficult. How do we get students to see that there are great writing topics inside and all around them? How do we teach children to add relevant details and write the kinds of stories that leave us satisfied, rather than confused and wanting something different? Before we can teach students the art of choosing topics and elaborating upon them, we need to lay a foundation for teaching and learning.

The Gradual Release of Responsibility Model

Growing up, I was a gymnast. While training, I frequently had to learn new tricks. My coach never told me, "Just do it." Instead, he went through a specific sequence to teach me new gymnastics tricks. First, he showed me, talking me through the steps to complete the stunt. Then I tried it, with careful hands spotting me through the trick. As I improved, my coach stepped back a little, spotting less and less, giving me feedback on how to improve. Finally, my coach let go. I practiced the trick on my own, over and over, sometimes falling, until finally I had mastered it.

My coach had used the "gradual release of

> ### STEPS IN THE GRADUAL RELEASE MODEL
> - Teacher modeling
> - Shared experience
> - Guided practice
> - Independent practice

responsibility" model of teaching (Pearson and Gallagher, 1983) without even knowing it. This is the model I, along with many teachers, use to teach students something new.

MODELED WRITING

While teaching writing, I always model first. I usually start with a piece of literature, and then I use my own writing. This allows me to show students something specific about writing. Students participate by looking, listening, and also commenting, but this method is very teacher-directed.

MODEL WITH LITERATURE For example, I may want to model how to "slow down a moment" by using one's senses to describe a scene, some action, or a character. *The Eyes of Gray Wolf* by Jonathan London is great to use as a model because it is filled with rich language.

I begin reading it, stopping to comment about writer's craft. "Look at how the author stretches this moment." I reread a sentence describing Gray Wolf's howl. Then I point out that the author doesn't stop here. He describes what the howl sounds like as it bounces "off the moon" and where the echo goes.

On another page I stop to let students notice the way London elaborates. After telling us that Gray Wolf senses danger, London goes on to tell what happens to the fur on the wolf's neck. The author adds more by telling what the wolf sees next. Because this book is packed with wonderful language, I reread it during another lesson to model the use of simile, metaphor, and personification as ways to elaborate.

Megan models writing for her students.

MODEL WITH TEACHER WRITING Books are our best models for what writers do, but students sometimes need to see writing in action. They need to watch someone think of a topic, elaborate on the topic, revise it for clarity, and edit it so it's as good as it can be. This is where the teacher comes in.

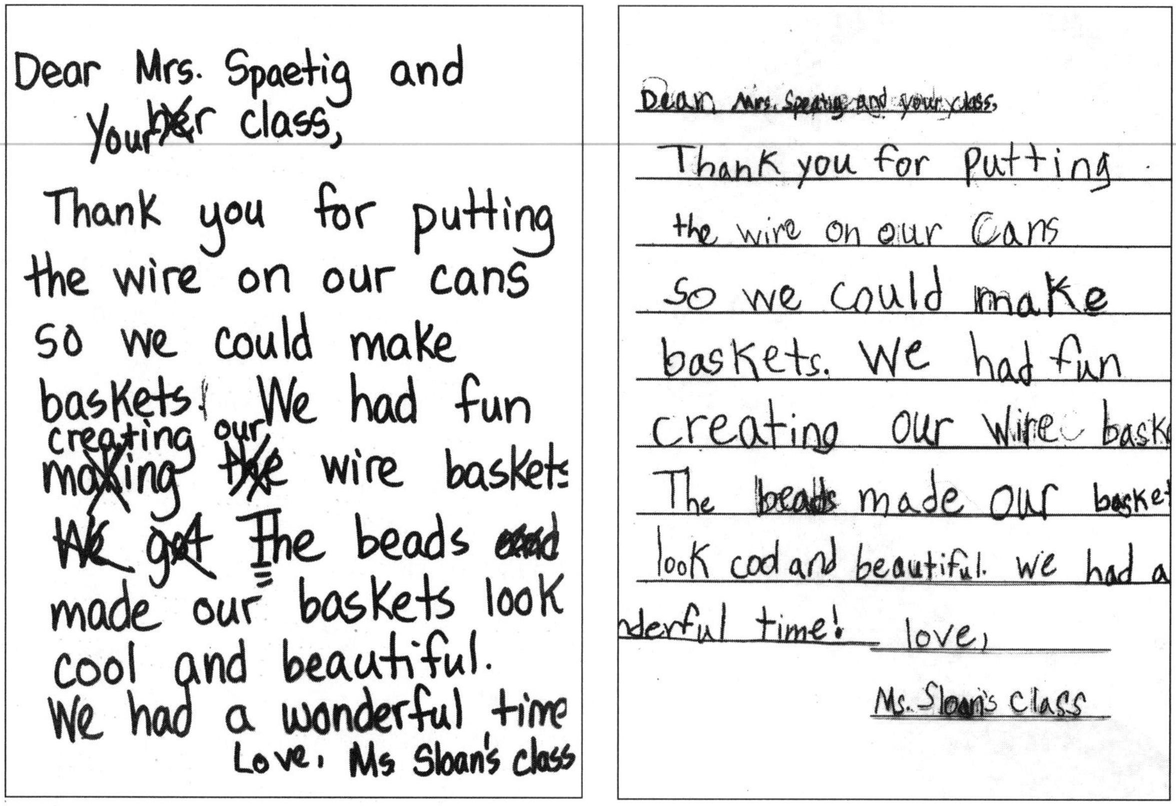

Dear Mrs. Spaetig and
Your~~her~~ class,
Thank you for putting
the wire on our cans
so we could make
baskets! We had fun
creating our ~~making the~~ wire baskets
~~We got~~ The beads ~~and~~
made our baskets look
cool and beautiful.
We had a wonderful time
Love, Ms Sloan's class

Dear Mrs. Spaetig and your class,
Thank you for putting
the wire on our Cans
so we could make
baskets. We had fun
creating our Wire bask
The beads made our baske
look cod and beautiful. We had a
nderful time! love,
Ms. Sloan's class

Figure 1.1
Shared writing of a thank-you letter (draft and rewrite).

I model writing for students every day. I pick my topics in front of them, thinking aloud about my possibilities. I add details, draw arrows to illustrate that writers add ideas even if there is no room, and revise to use more specific language. I show them that writers need to reread their writing as they write, not just afterward. When students see the process of writing a narrative, a nonfiction piece, or a poem, they understand better how to do it for themselves. When students see me work to elaborate on my ideas by describing what I see, hear, or feel, they have a better understanding of how to do this in their own writing.

SHARED WRITING

Shared writing is just that: sharing the writing. Both students and teacher contribute ideas. The teacher is usually the recorder and guides the writing of the group. This is a wonderful way to let go a little, while still holding onto the reins. Shared writing is a great way to teach elaboration, as well as other skills and strategies. Students participate in thinking of topics and using the various elaboration strategies they have learned. They then revise and edit. In my classroom, I use shared writing to model how to write thank-you (see Figure 1.1) and get-well letters to visitors or parent helpers, fiction stories, nonfiction pieces, poems, and biographies for our classroom library or the libraries of other classrooms. We write how-to guides for using school equipment and introduction books for new students. Students also decide how the writing should be published. A couple of students are chosen to rewrite neatly or type with correct conventions. Other students check their work before we send off our letter, poem, or book.

GUIDED PRACTICE AND INDEPENDENT WRITING

Now comes the shift. During guided practice, students are doing much more than the teacher. Writing about self-chosen topics, they practice the strategies I've taught in mini-lessons or modeled during shared writing. They may work alone or with peers. I let go. This does not mean that I don't keep a watchful eye on them. I ask questions. I tell them when I am confused by what they've written. I make suggestions. I confer with them so I can support them individually.

Take Joelle. I see that she is working very hard taking notes about different animals. She has been working for a day on this, so I decide to check in with her.

"Tell me what you are working on," I say as I pull up a stool.

Joelle answers, "I am taking notes about cheetahs."

"Oh, what have you learned so far?"

Joelle reads to me some of the facts she has learned.

I respond, "You have some very interesting facts here. What are you going to do with them?"

Joelle answers, "I'm going to make a book."

"That's a great idea. Tell me how you are going to organize it."

Joelle explains that each fact will go on its own page. Here is where I decide to check for learning. "Remember that we have been working on elaborating on ideas. Do you think you could take each fact and add to it?" I show her what I mean with one of the facts she has found. "Here, where you say 'Cheetahs run fast.' Could you tell a little more, like how fast they run, or why they need to run fast?"

Students writing independently.

Joelle confirms that she is planning on doing this. She says she will take each fact learned and add some details by giving some number facts (statistics) and telling why, how, and where.

I tell Joelle, "That is a great idea. I can't wait to check in with you again and see where you are with your book." Then I ask, "Do you need anything from me that would help you?" Joelle tells me that she might need help choosing which paper to use for her book. I tell her, "I will gladly help with that. When you are ready to make your book, let me know."

As we go from modeled to shared writing, and from guided to independent work, teacher responsibility declines and student responsibility rises. If the release is gradual, students are successful.

Teaching Within a Writing Workshop Structure

Teaching writing happens for me within a writing workshop. So what does that mean? According to Donald Graves, when setting up writing workshop in their classrooms, teachers should try to "discover the process they [real writers] go through and the reasons why they write. Then re-create those conditions in your own classrooms" (1994). During writing workshop, students go through various stages as they craft a piece of writing: pre-writing, drafting, revising, editing, and publishing

Regie Routman asks us to "think of it [writing workshop] as a time in which everything that writers do to create a meaningful piece of writing for a reader takes place." She includes self-chosen topics, writing with purpose and for an audience, conferring, and teaching as key elements (2005).

ORGANIZING WRITING WORKSHOP

Many people have the idea that writing workshop is an unstructured, "anything goes" kind of time in the classroom. Nothing could be further from the truth. It is a very structured time of day. I organize time in my writing workshop as shown in Figure 1.2.

Of course, the times may vary depending on grade level, time of year, and the amount of time a teacher has to devote to writing workshop. Though the times might vary from classroom to classroom, I believe the longest period should always be devoted to drafting or writing.

WRITING WORKSHOP
45–60 MINUTES

Mini-Lesson
5–15 minutes

Drafting and
Conferring
30–35
minutes

Sharing/Reflecting
10 minutes

Figure 1.2
A typical workshop schedule.

A QUICK PEEK My mini-lesson might include modeling the writing of something, while thinking aloud my process. It might include reading a piece of literature, nonfiction, or poetry, while pointing out what the author does well, such as elaboration. Or, I might engage students in a shared or interactive writing experience. Whichever the case, the lesson needs to be short, focusing on a few things for students to see and then possibly try.

Drafting and conferring is the longest period. Students need time to write and to practice what has been taught. This is how they will become good writers. This is also my time to confer one on one with children so that I know where they are and can discover ways to nudge them along.

Last, there's sharing and reflecting. Here, students reflect on what they've learned about themselves as writers. They also share parts or all of self-selected writing pieces. This is also our debriefing time, when we answer questions like: How did it go today? What will help us to work better tomorrow?

LINKING WRITING TO READING AND THE CONTENT AREAS

I try to weave writing workshop with reading workshop. If students are reading biographies, I encourage—and sometimes assign—them to research a famous person during reading and to write about this person during writing. When students reflect in reading journals about something read as a class, in a literature circle, or independently, I teach them to elaborate using the strategies they've learned (see Figure 1.3).

I also teach writing in the content areas. In math, when students solve a problem, I teach them to elaborate in their journals by telling how they solved it. What steps did they take? I also encourage self-reflection. Was it difficult? How did you feel while solving the problem? Did you ask for help from a classmate?

Our science journals include observations of small moments. While studying plants, students elaborate by describing, using

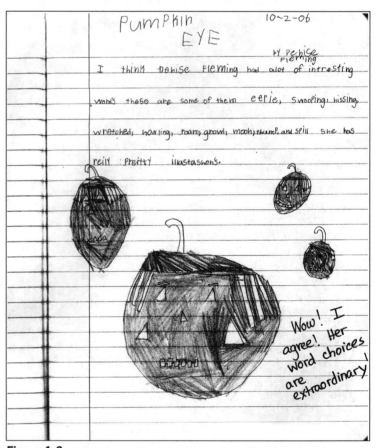

Figure 1.3

Mackenzie, a second grader, elaborates by using examples, while commenting on Denise Fleming's word choices in Pumpkin Eye.

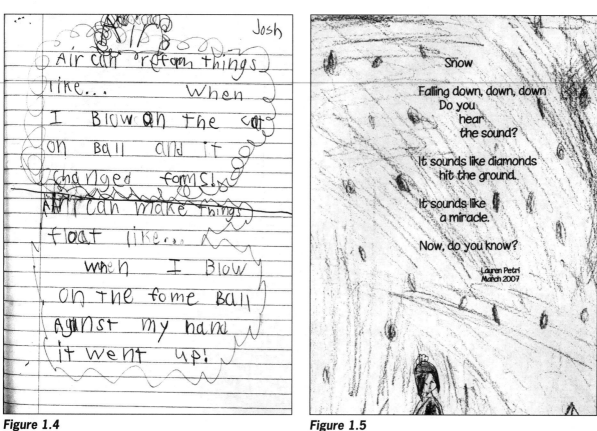

Figure 1.4
Josh uses examples in his writing about air in his science journal.

Figure 1.5
Lauren wrote a poem about snow.

statistics, and predicting growth. During our air and weather unit, students elaborate by giving examples and definitions of new terms (see Figure 1.4). This unit also spills over into writing workshop, as students write poems and stories about different kinds of weather such as rain, snow, and wind (see figures 1.5 and 1.6).

In social studies, as we study about communities with different geography, climate, and resources, students elaborate in journals by defining terms, giving examples, and telling their personal opinions about living in these different places. After learning about deserts, Johnny writes:

> Deserts can be harsh places. There is hardly any rain, making it hard for plants to grow. But some do, like the cactus.
>
> There are many animals that live in the desert; for example, scorpions, rattlesnakes, and roadrunners. They have to survive in the hot, dry, rocky environment.
>
> The largest desert is the Sahara. It is in Africa. Camels carry people and things across the hot sand. I'm not sure I could live in the desert. I would get thirsty.

Name Kenzie   Date 11-6-06

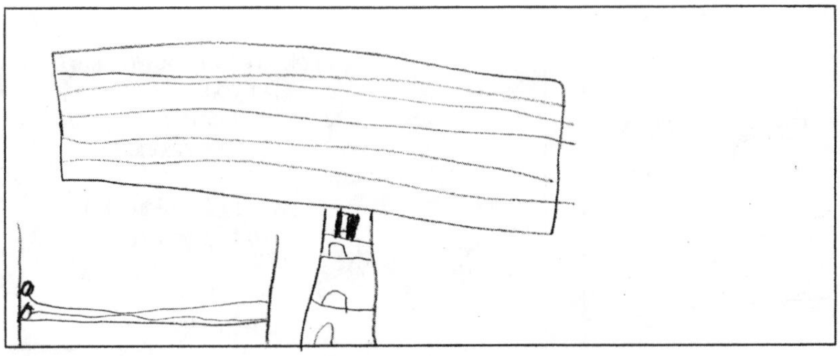

Rain can be a Pain

Rain can be a Pain beacause it can take thunder and lightning along with it. Like last night I hered the rain it seemd like it was saying im taking thunder and lighthing with me. I got scared and took my chair standed on it and got my two favrote blankets and

(4)

slept with them when I woke up in the middle of the night I called my mom and she slept with me I woke up in the middle of the night agian and woke my mom up and made her tern the light on caus the rain thunder and lightning went drip drop roar drip drop roar I went back to sleep when I woke up it was morning I got up got dressed brushed my teeth and my hair had breckfast left the haus with my unbrella got on the bus and got to shcool.

Figure 1.6
Mackenzie wrote about the rain.

First-grader Chase writes:

> **Deserts can be sandy. The sand is brown. The biggest sandy desert is the Sahara Desert.**

When we study people of history, Malcolm, a second grader, writes about Harriet Tubman.

HARRIET TUBMAN

Harriet Tubman was born in the early 1800s. Harriet was 29 when she escaped from slavery. She had an awfully mean master. Harriet's master whipped her and threw a weight at a slave, but it hit Harriet. She escaped on what they called the Underground Railroad.

The Underground Railroad wasn't really underground but they just called it that because it was secret. The houses were stations because there were white people who cared for the slaves and helped them escape slavery.

Harriet became a free woman. She went back nineteen times to save three hundred others. She was called a Moses to her people.

Harriet met Abe Lincoln and was a nurse and a spy during the Civil War. She helped many people. She lived a long life—to ninety-something. Harriet Tubman was a courageous woman!

Malcolm elaborates throughout the piece, giving specific details. He tells *how* the master was mean to Harriet. He also elaborates by defining the Underground Railroad and giving some facts about Tubman's trips back south and her age when she died.

Providing a Classroom Library of Models

I cannot say enough about the reading-writing connection. Making all kinds of books accessible to students (nonfiction, poetry, memoir, fiction, how-to manuals, biographies, and more) is very important. Students need chances to discover how other authors elaborate. Yes, they see this while I model with books, but I want them to discover ideas and topics on their own. I want them to notice how authors add details to their writing. I love it when students come to me and say, "Look, Mrs. Sloan, this author elaborated by adding a fact" or "Can I read this part of this book to the class? The author really slowed the moment down with details."

I want students to discover their favorite authors and be able to talk about the strategies these authors use to elaborate: describing; telling what someone says; or telling how, who, where, or why. Given lots of time with books, students will begin to borrow elaboration techniques from the greats like Patricia Polacco, James Marshall, and Charlotte Zolotow.

Creating a Community of Learners

When teaching writing, it is important that students feel safe. Writing requires risk-taking. Children need to develop enough confidence to write about meaningful topics. I remember Lacie, a student I had years ago. She was a first grader, new to our school. She was shy and uncertain about writing, never having done any writing in kindergarten. Lacie knew some letter names but few letter sounds. It was a struggle, but Lacie did become a confident writer. It took a lot of time and effort. First I let her just draw. Then I recorded her thoughts as she dictated them to me. Sometimes Lacie needed support in deciding what to draw or write. She loved rainbows and I remember her mom asking me, "Is she ever going to draw or write about anything else?"

My reply was, "Yes, when she is ready."

Lacie did draw rainbows for a few more weeks, occasionally adding a word or two to her picture such as "mom" or "dad" or "Lacie," and then one day, without warning, she drew her new house and wrote: "I got a new house." It took a lot of courage for Lacie to switch topics. She was comfortable with rainbows. But, just as I told her mom, she changed topics when she was ready.

I remember another student, Brian, a child of a single mom. He did not see his dad

Figure 1.7
Lacie writes about her house.

16

very often and this bothered Brian. We were reading *Ereth's Birthday* by Avi. In the book, the porcupine, Ereth, takes care of three fox kits when their mother is killed. The kits have a father, but he does not come around very often.

This book prompted Brian, a third grader, who hated writing and also lacked many writing skills, to write. He took out his reading journal and wrote the following response:

> **I know how the kits feel. I miss my dad too. I don't see him very much. I wish I did. I would do lots of things with him, like play video games and watch movies.**

Ralph Fletcher says, "Writing with real honesty takes tremendous courage" (1993). I believe it took great courage for Brian to write about this very personal topic. I also believe it took Lacie equal courage to write when she had never written before and was uncertain about letter sounds. So, how do we create an environment to foster risk taking and a love for writing? We do so by getting to know our students and letting them get to know us.

TELLING MY STORIES AND SHARING MY WRITING

One way I try to help students like Lacie feel comfortable about writing is by letting them know who I am. They know my favorite books, my favorite TV shows. They know I like to travel, and that I have two nieces who live nearby. I tell students my stories so that they get to know me, but also so that they will begin to tell their stories. These stories will become their writing.

I write in front of students and share bits of my journal, so they can see that I struggle to get things right, add enough detail, or choose the right words. I share a piece I am proud of, as well as one I never finished.

"I have a piece of writing from my journal that I would like to share with you today." I remind students that my mom had a stroke and that she is different from how she was before. Of course, students are eager to listen.

I read:

My mom had a stroke. She is different from how she was before. She knows me but she has forgotten a lot. The other day we had a short but wonderful conversation. She remembered when we were young, living in Virginia. Five of her seven children were playing in the front yard. I was there along with Mike, Bill, Tom, and Kate. She couldn't remember what we were playing, but she said we were laughing and having fun.

I thought back to living in that house in Fairfax, Virginia, my mom so young and active, focused on her family. I pictured us all playing in the front yard. I heard children's laughter.

So many years have gone by. My mom now has wrinkles; so do I. It is a long time since that day in Fairfax, Virginia, but it feels like yesterday.

After reading, I tell students that this conversation with my mom happened yesterday. "I'm not sure I'm happy with the way I wrote it. Perhaps I should make it a poem instead," I say. "I think I will keep this, and continue to make changes until it feels right. I think I can add more specific details and maybe change some words so it sounds better."

In this lesson I talk and write about a very important topic: my mom. I am vulnerable in front of students. I show them how I struggle to get the words and sentences right. I want students to see that if they care about their topics, they will be committed to their writing; they will want it to be good.

If students see that I am willing to open up my life in my writing, maybe they will too. If students see that I have challenges, as well as successes in writing, they will feel more comfortable as we work together to both improve and celebrate their writing.

GETTING TO KNOW MY STUDENTS

Knowing your students takes time, but is so important in teaching writing. I want to know the likes and dislikes of students. What do they like to read about? Maybe those are the topics they will choose to write about. Is there a science buff in the class? Who likes to dance? Is there someone in the class who has a unique hobby? I can make suggestions and ask good questions if I know students' interests.

I also want to know students' perceptions and backgrounds in writing. Did they write much last year? Do they dislike writing or are they like Mackenzie, who keeps a journal at home and can't stop writing? If writing is a chore for a student, I need to work extra hard to make him engage in lessons and apply strategies he's learned. I need to work to make him see the power of writing. If students love writing, I need to help them become better, showing lots of different ways to elaborate, organize, and format their writing.

CREATING A RESPECTFUL AND HELPFUL ENVIRONMENT

As we get to know each other, we establish promises for our lessons, drafting time, and sharing. Students learn to trust one another because we treat each other with respect. Here are the promises we make:

1. We listen and participate in writing lessons.
2. We respect everyone's ideas.
3. We write quietly and honor that this is a thinking time.
4. We help each other.
5. We listen and participate in sharing our writing and giving feedback to classmates.

Of course we practice these things. We make mistakes along the way, but we always come back to these promises. Students know that our classroom is a safe place to share, ask questions, and celebrate their writing.

Knowing About Writing

Ralph Fletcher says, "Writing teachers draw upon three areas of expertise. We must know our students. We must know how to teach. And we must know something about writing itself" (1993). I could not agree more. I've spoken about knowing students and knowing how to teach; now we come to knowing about writing.

Teachers need to learn about what makes good writing, as well as the process writers follow to write something worth reading. We need to read work by Donald Murray, Regie Routman, Donald Graves, Lucy Calkins, and Ralph Fletcher. We need to be able to point out what works in a picture book or in a paragraph in a chapter book. Does the author use descriptions that make you feel as if you're there? Does she elaborate by telling what someone says or feels? Does the author use language that invites us further into the text? Does she write a lead and an ending that serve as bookends so the piece can stand alone?

In addition, we need to understand the writing process, knowing that writers are individuals; none of them follows the exact plan of another. When talking to published authors, I find that some take extensive notes before beginning to write. Others start writing, stop to take notes, and then continue writing again. I recently asked Avi, "How many hours a day do you write?" He told me it was hard to gauge. He suspected about eight to ten hours, but he said that includes thinking. For him (and I couldn't agree more), "writing is thinking."

Some writers draft solely on the computer; others write on a pad. When I write, I do both. I start in longhand on a pad. I revise along the way. When I think I have a large enough chunk, I type on the computer, continuing to revise. Then I continue writing on the computer, more revising, and go back to my pad again. Most writers visit each of the stages of the writing process (prewrite, draft, revise, edit, publish) over and over again.

Final Thoughts

If we want to be good writing teachers, we must make sure we treat students like individuals as they write, honoring their styles. Maybe Johnny needs to draw an extensive picture before writing. Emma likes to start right in, drawing a picture later. Tyler needs to sit and think for about five minutes. Chase likes to lie on the floor with his notebook and write.

In addition, we must know what makes good writing. And then we must teach intentionally. After that we need to let students have a go, struggle to get it right, and practice—and then celebrate what they have learned.

CHAPTER 2

FINDING TOPICS, NARROWING TOPICS, AND STAYING FOCUSED

I've just finished a lesson in writing workshop, and it's time for students to begin their own writing. Everyone is moving around the room getting paper, taking out writing folders, and finding a space to sit and write. As the buzz quiets, I notice Michael (usually an eager writer) sitting with a blank piece of paper and an equally blank stare. I pull up my stool and ask Michael, "What are you thinking about?"

He answers with the dreaded, "I don't know what to write about."

At first I think, "Oh, no—we could be here for a while." But then my mind races to recent events and I say, "Michael, didn't your mom have a baby yesterday?"

He looks up at me with wide eyes. "Oh yeah!" he responds excitedly, and off he starts writing, needing no more help from me.

Learning to Choose Topics That "Fit"

I would like to say it is always so easy: I nonchalantly make suggestions to a stumped writer and all of a sudden he or she is off and running. But that's not always the case. Take Tyler, for instance, a boy I worked with a few years ago. Tyler was smart. He loved to read. Despite that, he came into my third-grade classroom with an IEP for reading and writing. Tyler could read above his grade level with deep understanding of text. What he could not do was write about it. We quickly dismissed his reading IEP, but he still had a valid IEP for written language. Tyler hated writing about anything. He could write if he set his mind to it, but he struggled. Tyler was a great thinker, but getting him to put even one idea on paper was a battle. When Tyler said, "I don't know what to write about," he meant it, and all of the brainstorming I might do with him over a 30-minute period would still result in a boy without an idea, with a blank sheet of paper.

Then there's the child who is willing to write, but just can't think of topics. He is always the one at the beginning of writing workshop, looking around the room with unsure eyes. He has that half-frown, doubting that he has any idea interesting enough to keep him, the writer, focused, and us, the readers, interested. He wants to write, but lacks the confidence to commit to an idea. He always comes up empty-handed and depends on the help of the teacher to choose his topic.

How do we help children like these discover topics? How do we help them see that there is an abundance of rich ideas around them?

CONNECTING TO TEXT: THINKING ABOUT TOPICS TO WRITE ABOUT One of my favorite books for helping students find topics is *You Have to Write* by Janet Wong. It is a wonderful text for exemplifying that a student's own life is a great place to begin when searching for ideas. Wong urges the reader to write. She suggests that it is in our nature to write, that we must tell our stories and the stories of our mothers, fathers, grandparents, and so on. She says we want readers to laugh or cry at our words. Wong seems to go inside the head of the reluctant writer who wants to be a writer, but just can't seem to believe she can come up with that topic that will wow everyone.

The illustrator of Wong's book, Teresa Flavin, created little snapshots of everyday activities: a birthday party, a walk in the rain, cookie-baking with Dad. On the same page Wong asks the reader, "Who else can say what you have seen? Who else can tell your stories?" Immediately, the reader sees that writing can be telling stories about her life and the lives of those around her. Most young students are interested in themselves, so getting them to write about their lives usually takes only a slight nudge.

I read this book to students and we talk about the everyday topics that might inspire us. We make a chart of ideas, and I encourage students to think of the ordinary, and the not-so-ordinary, things in their own lives that will make good stories (see Figure 2.1).

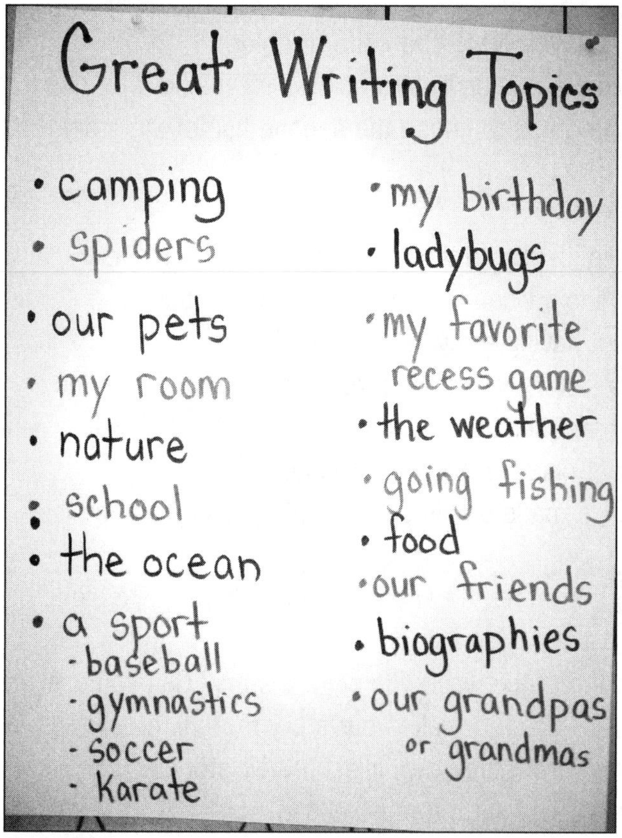

Figure 2.1
Our chart of student-generated ideas.

FINDING A TOPIC USING LITERATURE AS A MODEL

Wong's message resonates with many students. They want to write about their lives. Some students, however, are still not sure. This is when I introduce *Flip's Fantastic Journal* by Angelo DeCesare. In this book, a dog is asked to write in his journal about his life. He begins to write, but reluctantly, because he finds his life to be quite boring and unlucky. It is clear that Flip does not like to write. He says so. But he does his homework, dutifully. He writes, but what he writes is quite dull. Then Flip has an idea. He remembers his teacher saying he doesn't have to write about his real day, and inviting him to make things up. All of a sudden, Flip twists his real events into more exciting happenings, and these new and exciting happenings are now illustrated in color. What used to be Flip hitting himself in the head with the soccer ball turns into Flip kicking the soccer ball to the moon. What used to be a cereal box with no toy inside becomes a cereal box filled with toys. This is Flip's life, exaggerated toward the positive. After reading the book, I ask students, "So what do you think?"

Tyler says, "I like how the book went from black-and-white to color."

"Yes. That was pretty neat. Why did the author/illustrator do this?" I ask.

Jessica answers, "Because he wanted you to notice the second half of the story is much more interesting."

I ask, "In what way?"

Tatum begins, "In the beginning, Flip just listed the things he did. It wasn't very interesting. Then, in the middle of the book, when he started over, Flip made up things, like instead of his cereal box not having a toy, it was full of toys."

Michael adds, "Yeah, and when his sister woke him up early in the morning in the first half, you could tell he didn't like that. Then in the second half he says his sister tried to wake him up, but he told his pet dinosaur to get her instead."

I agree, "I get what you're saying. He made up his story in the second half and it was more interesting?"

Miya says, "Yes. But he used things from his life and then made them seem bigger and better."

I ask, "Do you think this is a good technique when you write a story? Can you use things from your own life and exaggerate them to make your story more interesting? Do you think authors of fiction use things from their own lives in their stories?"

Students nod their heads and a few shout out, "Yes!"

Memoirs in Literature

I tell students, "You know, one of the masters at taking moments from her life and stretching them into stories, and perhaps filling in the gaps with fictional ideas, is Patricia Polacco. Many of her stories are about things she experienced at some time in her life, a lot of them when she was a child."

At this time, I introduce the book, *Thank You, Mr. Falker* by Patricia Polacco. I read the story and as I do, students are outraged by how the main character is treated. She cannot read and the boys tease her. But her teacher never gives up. He believes in her, and listeners are swept into the story, really caring about whether this child learns to read. At the end, of course, we all get a surprise. We find out who this little girl is: no other than the author of the book, Patricia Polacco.

As I close the book, I ask students to look at this story through writers' eyes. "What do you think? What did you think of her topic?"

"I think it was a good topic because it was about her," says Tayler.

"Yes, that was a surprise at the end to find out Patricia Polacco had a hard time learning to read and now she is a wonderful author!"

"So this story is about her life?" asks Johnny.

"Yes. She might have been like Flip, adding things to make this story, but she got the idea from her own life."

"Patricia Polacco has written a memoir. A memoir is when an author writes about a specific memory or time in his or her life.

Joelle says, "So, we can write memoirs too?"

"Yes, you might when you write about your life," I answer.

I ask students to consider using their own lives as springboards for writing topics. Think about the "moments" of time. Maybe it is a day, or a week, or just a few minutes of time. Perhaps you found a hermit crab under a beach rock, or were caught in a bad rainstorm. Maybe your dog finally learned the new trick you were teaching him. Remember these moments and write about them. They will make great topics!

◆

MINI-LESSON

MODELING CHOOSING A TOPIC

One of the things I want to show students is that authors consider many topics before they write. Often, they have notes on many ideas that might make a good book. They look for a "good fit." By that I mean a topic that inspires and nudges the writer to write. At a recent visit to Western Washington University, Avi, author of many books including *Crispin: The Cross of Lead*, *The True Confessions of Charlotte Doyle*, and *Poppy*, said that he works on several books at the same time. While this might seem overwhelming to us, we all do this on a small scale. We often write many things during a day: e-mails, letters, essays, poems, lists, proposals, and more.

The hard part for students should not be coming up with an idea for writing, but narrowing their ideas to one for right now. I love it when students say, "But I want to write about two things."

I say, "Great! Pick one now and let's write your other idea down so you can write about it later."

I gather students together and tell them, "I am not sure what I will write about today. Let me think." I pause. "I could write about watching the Mariners game the other day with my dad." I jot that down on the top corner of my chart. I show students I am thinking again. Then I add, "Or I could write about last night. I was snuggled up in bed reading a really good book." I add that to the corner of the chart. Then I say, "Oh, I have another idea. I went to see my friend's daughter pole vault on Saturday." Again, I write that idea down.

I look at my choices and say, "You know, I think I will write about going to see Alexa pole vault." I put a star by that idea and tell my story to students. Then I begin to write. As I write, I stop and show my thinking. I make changes. As I reread, I revise and edit. I end up with a short piece about my experience on Saturday.

The next day, I reread my piece to students. I tell them, "You know, it was not hard to write about this topic because I really knew about it. I also really enjoyed seeing Alexa pole vault. Both of those things made it a good topic for me. It was a good fit. When authors pick topics, they have to be sure they have something to say about their idea."

Then I launch into a "nonexample" of a good topic. I tell students, "Today, I think I will write about Russia."

I begin writing, and it is very clear, very fast, that I have run out of things to say.

Russia is a country in Europe. I hear it is cold there. I would like to go to St. Petersburg.

After writing two lines, I stop and say, "Wow. I can't think of anything else to say. I guess I don't know much about Russia. I have never been there, and I haven't read any books about it. I guess Russia is not a very good topic for me."

I compare my piece about Russia with the one I wrote about watching Alexa pole vault. "I didn't have any problem writing about Alexa, but I did have a problem thinking of ideas to write about Russia. What was the difference?"

Jill says, "You have never seen Russia, but you've seen Alexa pole vault."

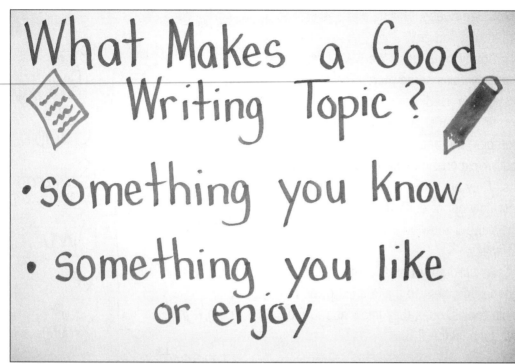

Figure 2.2
Our class chart about good writing topics.

I respond, "You're right. I know about going to see Alexa pole vault because I experienced it. Good topics are ones we know about."

I add, "I also liked seeing Alexa pole vault. I really enjoyed myself, so I guess good topics are ones that you like or enjoy."

We make a chart entitled: What Makes a Good Topic? (see Figure 2.2).

You know, it's like Cinderella's slipper. A good topic just fits. A bad topic is like trying to squish my foot into a shoe that is too small or placing it into a shoe that is too big. Just like the shoe, a topic that fits me might not fit you, and vice versa. It can be very personal.

I encourage students to pick topics they know and like. These will be the best fit topics for them. I ask, "Who thinks they have a good topic for themselves?"

Tatum answers, "I'm going to write about my dog."

"That's a good topic, Tatum. You certainly know about your dog, and you always talk about him, so I know you like him. I think you will find a lot to say about that topic. Anyone else?"

Jarred says, "I'm going to write about the weather because I really know about the weather. I felt the wind and I watched it blow the leaves off the trees today."

"It sounds like that is an interesting topic for you, as well," I say. Jarred nods. "Who else has an idea?"

Bobby raises his hand and says, "I went camping over the weekend."

I urge Bobby, "Tell us about it. Where did you go?"

Bobby continues, "We went over the mountains somewhere. There was a lake. We used a tent this time."

"Well, you should know about your camping trip because you experienced it. Our experiences are ready-made topics. They are ones in which the details just flow out of our pencils and onto the page. I know you would have a lot to say."

As children go off to write, I encourage them to make a list of possible topics, ones they know about and like (see Figure 2.3).

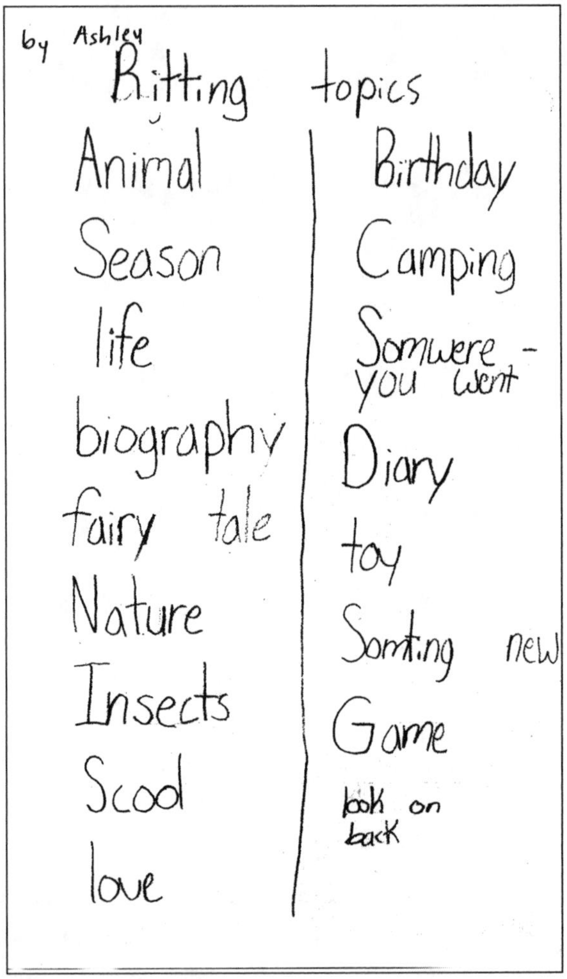

Figure 2.3
Student-generated topic list.

Narrowing Topics

One of the greatest problems students have is narrowing their topics. It is easy for students to write about their weekends: "On Saturday I got up and watched cartoons. Then we went to my baseball game. We won. After that we went to McDonalds. That night we watched movies at my friend's house. We watched *Shrek*. I really like that movie. It's one of my favorites. On Sunday we had a barbecue and then I did my homework Sunday night." This is very boring. It is called a bed-to-bed story. It is a list of things void of any elaboration or detail. How do we help students zero in on the most important part of their story?

NARROWING A TOPIC

To teach about narrowing one's topic, I decide to model again. I have written my piece out ahead of time, to save time for the real work we will do today.

"Boys and girls, I want to share my piece of writing with you. I wrote it this morning." I share the following piece:

On Saturday I had a busy day. I had to run errands in the morning. Then I went to my sister's house and played with my nieces. We watched a movie too. Afterward I went downtown and had ice cream. I had vanilla swirl. It was still light, so we went over to the baseball field to watch a game. The Red team won. It was a fun day.

After reading my piece, I say, "You know, I told you a lot of things, but I didn't really elaborate on any one of them. It's like I just listed the things I did on Saturday without going into any detail. I'm thinking I tried to include too many ideas. Maybe I should narrow my topic."

Lauren asks, "What does that mean?"

I explain, "*Narrow* means to get smaller. When I say I need to narrow my topic, it means I need to write about less, maybe just one of my ideas, but explain more about that one idea."

"In this case, I tried to tell you too many things. I should pick one and just focus on that." I reread my piece and decide to narrow my topic to just the baseball game. I circle that part of my writing. Then I say, "I could tell you about the whole game, or I could just tell you about the last inning, when all the excitement happened. That's what I think I will do." I write in front of students, thinking aloud as I write.

It was a pretty exciting game. The score was tied and it was the last inning. The pitcher had already walked one batter and struck one batter out. One player was on first base. The crowd was cheering and as the tall, lanky player walked toward the plate, the air was filled with tension.

"Strike one!" the umpire yelled. The batter stepped back, spat in the dirt, and swung his bat back over his shoulder.

The pitch came and he hit a pop fly to center field. It was caught. Some cheered. Some moaned.

Here we were: the next batter—who might be the last batter in the game. All of the Red team's hopes were in this kid. He took a few hardy warm-up swings and stepped to the plate. Smack! You could hear the ball hit the catcher's glove. "Strike one!" yelled the umpire. The batter looked toward his coach at third base. A secret message was signaled. The batter stepped forward again. Smack! "Strike two!" yelled the ump again. A hush fell over the Red side's bleachers.

The batter stepped back, readjusted his hands to the bat, and dug his feet into the dirt. The sun was setting. This was it. This was their last chance to win. I looked out at the scoreboard.

The pitch came. The batter swung. Crack! Bat hit ball. It sailed out toward right field. The runner on first ran, fast as lightning. Both runners had rounded second. One was at third and one was headed toward home plate. The catcher was crouched low, ready to catch the long-thrown ball and tag the runner out. The ball was thrown. The runner sped. He slid his legs under the catcher's feet, just as the ball was caught. "SAFE!" yelled the umpire. Cheers echoed through my ears, along with long, low "Noooos" from the opposing side. The game was over. The Red team won!

Depending on the age of students, I might shorten this piece, or perhaps write it on my own and bring it back to my students the next day.

I ask students, "What do you think?"

Lauren says, "That is a lot better than your first story. It was more interesting."

"What made it more interesting? Did narrowing the topic help?" Students agree that it helped to just write about baseball and forget the other ideas. They also liked that I didn't write about the whole game, just the last inning. I explain that it is really important to write about what sticks out in your mind, rather than listing off all of the things you can think of. I tell students, "I always say, 'Write a lot about a little.' Take a small topic and elaborate upon that. For instance, if you want to write about your favorite place, don't say, 'the fair.' Ask yourself, 'Where at the fair?' Don't say 'the Ferris wheel'. Say, 'at the top of the Ferris wheel where it feels like I can see the whole world.'"

"A colleague of mine, Kary Thome, once had a student who loved baseball. He wrote about his favorite place, but he didn't say it was the baseball field. He wrote, 'My favorite place is behind the fearless mask of the catcher.' He went on to explain the game from that point of view. Now, THAT is narrowing one's topic!"

I ask students to think about narrowing their topics today. "If you are going to write about your weekend, or a camping trip, or a baseball game, try to figure out which moment stands out. Then write about that. Maybe you caught a frog on your camping trip. Write about that. Maybe you went to a birthday party. Write about just one part of the party. Think about what would make an interesting story." (See Figure 2.4.)

Staying Focused on Your Topic

Another problem students have is starting with one topic and going off to another in the same piece. They begin writing about fall and all of a sudden, it becomes a piece about football. In testing situations, this is referred to as "off prompt." However, I see this even when students choose their own topics. They find it hard to keep focused.

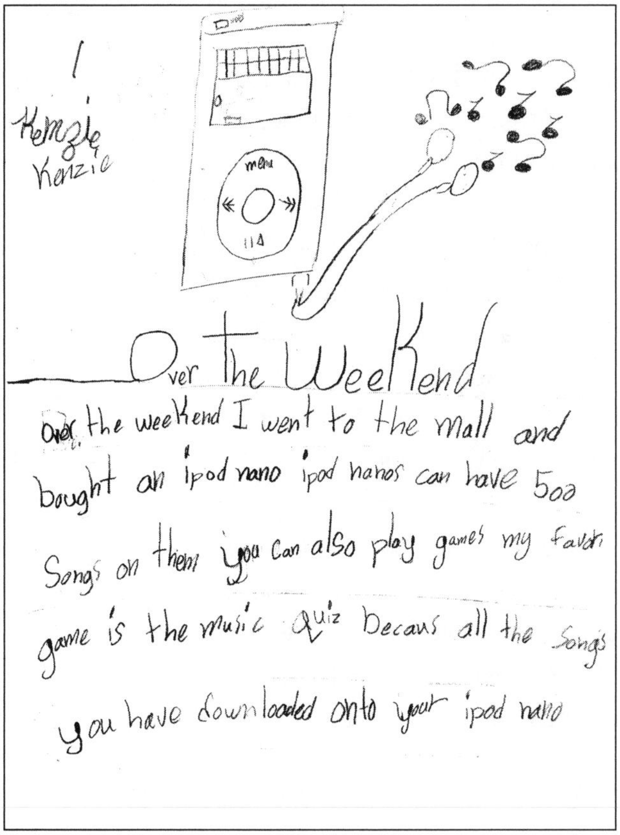

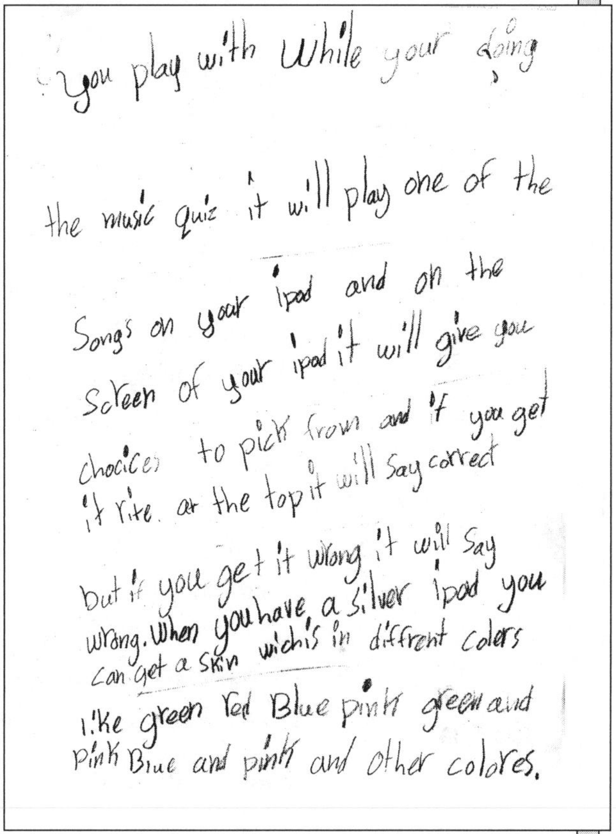

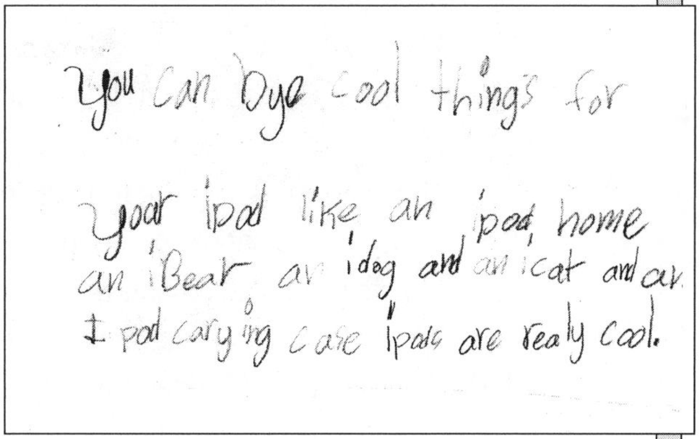

Figure 2.4
Mackenzie, a second grader, narrows her topic to iPods. Instead of writing about the whole mall experience, she just tells us about her iPod.

ONE-TO-ONE IN FRONT OF THE CLASS

I decide to give a prompt, asking students to tell about their favorite season and explain why it is their favorite. Ashley, a second grader, chooses summer and writes in her three-page piece shown in Figure 2.5.

Ashley is a solid writer with many strengths: her lead and ending sentences, her descriptions, and her language. It seems to me Ashley just lost her focus for a while, and she even notices it ("Now, back to what I like about summer").

The day after students write to this prompt, I settle in for a follow-up lesson. I tell students that I am very impressed with their writing. "You have learned to use many of the elaboration techniques I have taught. I see interesting language and wonderful lead and ending sentences. There is, however, one area I see some students need help with, and that is staying focused on your topic. Some of you began writing about your season and then when you started to elaborate, you lost your way. One of the details became the whole story and your piece was no longer about your favorite season."

"If you write about summer, and you tell about dirt biking in the summer, that has to be a part, rather than your whole piece turning into Why I Love Dirt Biking. It's okay to write about dirt biking. That might be a great topic for you. But remember, this topic for this assignment was your favorite season."

Ashley raises her hand, "I think I did that. I started to write too much about horses and I got off my topic about summer."

I ask Ashley if she would like to share her writing with the class. We project her piece onto the screen.

Ashley reads her piece aloud. I ask her, "Tell me what you are thinking."

She responds, "I started to talk about horses too much. I should take that part out."

I say, "Show me where." Ashley points to the sentence, "They have horses."

I ask her to read from there until she finishes the part about horses. I prod, "Do you think all of this should be edited out or just some of it?"

Ashley thinks for a minute. She is silently rereading this part again. "Well," she says, "Maybe the part about their names is okay because that is a detail. But when I start telling about the horses moving—that is too much."

"Okay, let's try taking that out." I cover that section and ask Ashley to reread her entire piece, eliminating that part about the horses. After she reads, I ask, "What do you think?"

"I like it better," she answers.

"Why?"

She responds, "Because it's all about summer now."

I ask the class to tell us what they think. They all agree with Ashley.

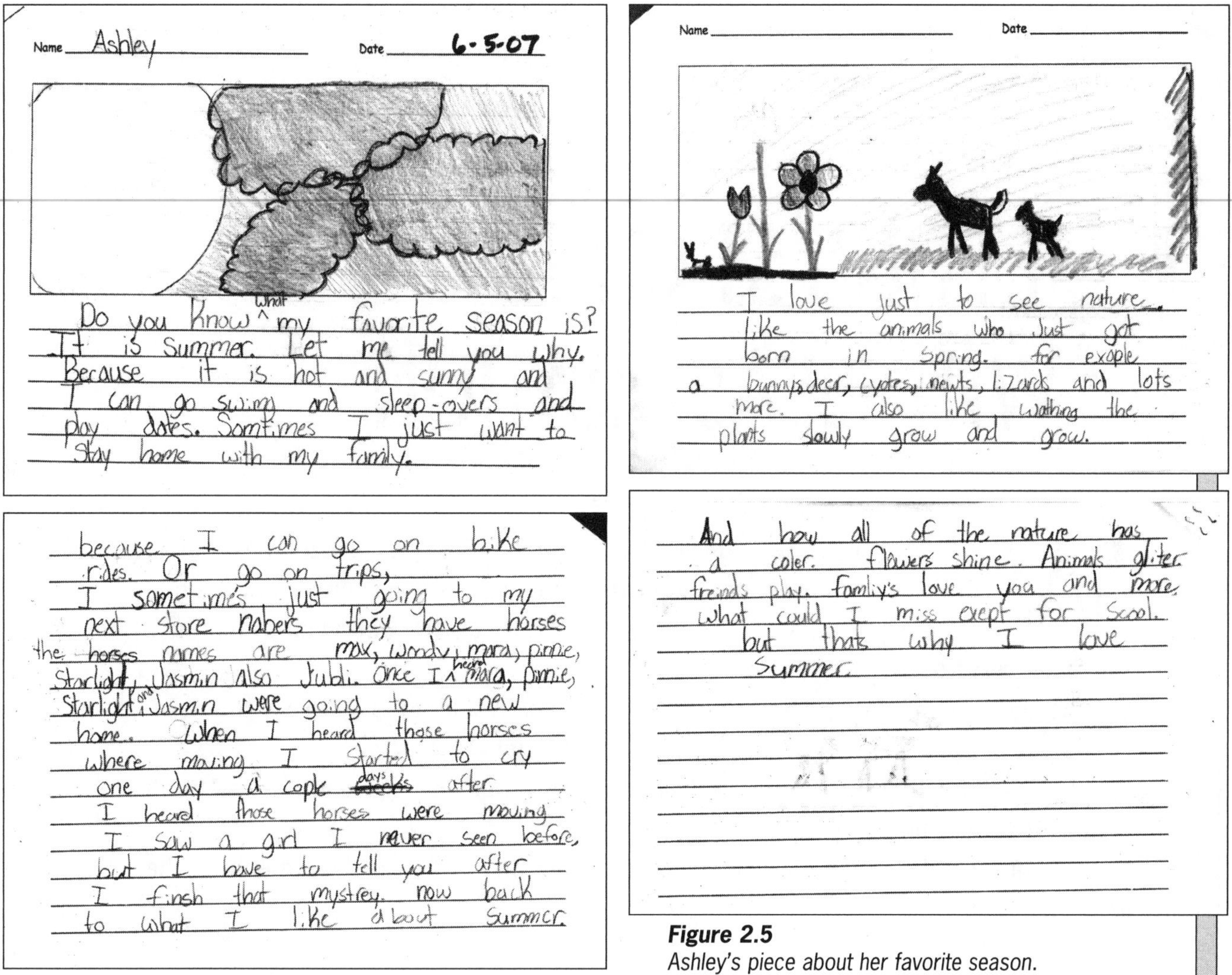

Name Ashley   Date 6-5-07

Do you know ^What my favorite season is? It is summer. Let me tell you why. Because it is hot and sunny and I can go swim and sleep-overs and play dates. Somtimes I just want to stay home with my family.

Name ___   Date ___

I love just to see nature. Like the animals who just got born in spring. for exople a bunnys, deer, cyotes, newts, lizards and lots more. I also like wathing the plants slowly grow and grow.

because I can go on bike rides. Or go on trips, I sometimes just going to my next store nabers they have horses the horses names are max, wandy, mara, pinne, Starlight, Jasmin also Jubi. Once I heard mara, pinne, Starlight and Jasmin were going to a new home. When I heard those horses where moving I started to cry one day a cople days after I heard those horses were moving I saw a girl I never seen before, but I have to tell you after I finsh that mystery. now back to what I like about Summer.

And how all of the nature has a coler. flowers shine. Animals gliter freinds play. famliy's love you and more. what could I miss exept for scool. but thats why I love Summer.

Figure 2.5
Ashley's piece about her favorite season.

"You know," I begin, "sometimes we need to revise by taking things out of our writing, but we can save those lines for another story. Ashley, do you think you might like to write about your neighbor's horses sometime? If so, you might use this part because it is really good. It just didn't fit here in this piece".

I encourage students to reread their pieces to see if there is a place where they went off topic. I hold individual conferences over the next several days to talk with students about staying focused on their favorite-season writing. I will address more about one-on-one conferences in Chapter 7.

Final Thoughts

Teaching students to discover topics that are personally relevant is very important. Children write better if they know and love what they write about. Once students choose their topics, helping them to narrow and stay focused becomes the challenge. However, through modeling and one-on-one conferences, you can show them how to choose topics, stay focused on one or two ideas, and elaborate upon them in their writing.

CHAPTER 3

GETTING STARTED WITH ELABORATION

We are all familiar with this classroom scene: First-grader Katie has drawn a picture of a brown dog. She reads to me what she has written at the bottom of the page: "I have a dog." When I ask Katie, "Do you want to tell more?" she answers, "No, that's all."

"Really," I try again. "I notice your dog is brown. Would you like to say that too?" Katie pauses, and I think, "She's going to add a detail."

"No," she finally says. "I'm done." No amount of pushing or prodding, no "Don't you want to add more?" is going to help.

So, once a child has an idea, how do we inspire him or her to elaborate upon that idea—to tell more?

Defining Elaboration

New Lexicon Webster's Encyclopedic Dictionary defines *elaborate* as "to make or develop with care, to work out in detail . . . to go into details about a matter." In *6 + 1 Traits of Writing: The Complete Guide, Grades 3 and Up*, Ruth Culham includes *elaborating* as a key piece (the developmental piece) of the ideas trait (2003). For me, *elaborate* simply means to *tell more*. This is the definition I use with my young students because it's the one they will understand. *Elaborate* is one of the first new words I introduce to students. We talk about it. We post on the wall:

ELABORATE = TELL MORE

I want this word to become part of my students' working vocabulary, so we need to ask the question: What does it mean to elaborate or tell more? How do we tell more?

⚷ CONNECTING TO TEXT I begin with what I know works: real literature. If I want students to elaborate, I need to first show it, and then define it. So we turn to books, some of my first graders' favorites, including *In the Small, Small Pond* by

Denise Fleming, *Stellaluna* by Janell Cannon, *Deserts* by Gail Gibbons, and our current read-aloud, *Poppy* by Avi.

We read from each, stopping to notice how the author tells more. Fleming begins her story by telling of a "small, small pond . . . ." As we turn each page, she answers our recurring question—"What else?"—by telling us about new pond creatures, including new language to describe how each moves.

In *Stellaluna*, Janell Cannon tells more by telling *how*. She says that Stellaluna is learning to be like the birds and then explains how Stellaluna does this: by staying awake in the daytime and sleeping at night. Cannon goes on to tell us that Stellaluna eats bugs, regardless of their terrible taste.

I ask students, "What is the author telling us about Stellaluna?"

Josh answers, "That she learned to be like birds."

"Yes," I answer. "Does the author tell more?"

Tatum says, "Yes, she tells us she stays awake in the day and sleeps at night."

Adena adds, "And she eats bugs now, even though they taste bad."

I continue, "When the author does this, she's really telling more by *telling how*. Janell Cannon tells us Stellaluna learned to be like the birds, and then she adds details to tell us *how* she learned to be like birds: that she stayed awake in the day and slept at night, and that she ate bugs."

In *Deserts*, Gail Gibbons tells more by describing what sandy deserts look like. She begins telling us that sandy deserts look different from other deserts. She compares the sand to rippling water. She describes the way wind changes the sand's appearance by blowing it this way and that, piling it into big, smooth hills.

Gibbons also tells more by telling why rocky deserts look strange. She describes the way wind wears down the rocks, making them look peculiar. Rain cuts into the rocks, making them jagged, and heat and cold can make the rock break away.

Again, I nudge students to notice how the author elaborates. "What does Gail Gibbons tell us about rocky deserts?"

Alex says, "They can look strange."

"Right," I say. "How does she elaborate on that idea?"

Miya answers, "She tells us how the rocks got that way . . . why they look strange . . . the wind blows the sand and it wears the rocks into different shapes."

"Yes. She is telling us more by telling us why—specifically, why the rocks came to look strange. That's another way of telling more, or elaborating."

And in *Poppy*, Avi describes the Old Orchard the mouse must cross, elaborating by telling what she sees all around her.

> *Even better, the grass was high among the old twisted apple trees, providing good camouflage. Here and there delicate pink lady's slippers bloomed. Berry bushes were heavy with fruit. Bluebirds, jays, and warblers flitted by. Grasshoppers leaped about joyfully.*

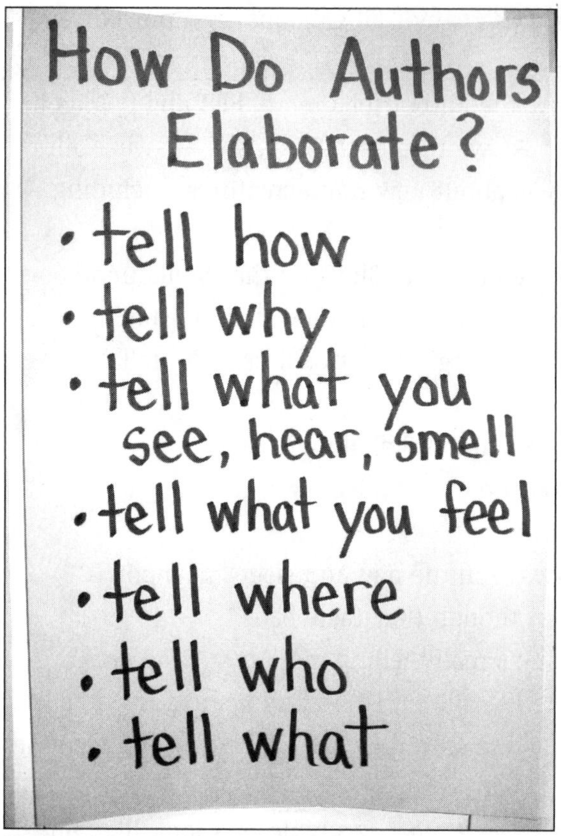

Figure 3.1
As a class, we made a chart about how authors elaborate.

How Do Authors Elaborate?

• tell how
• tell why
• tell what you see, hear, smell
• tell what you feel
• tell where
• tell who
• tell what

I LIK TO PLA N MI

STKR BSH FRT YITH

TRSHU I SIT DN WE

ET DONTS.

Figure 3.2
Ashley elaborates by telling where, who, and what.

When I read this passage, we speak about how Avi tells more by describing everything around Poppy—telling what she sees. Again, I point out that this is another way authors tell more—by telling what a character sees. See pages 35–38 for more examples from literature.

As I read aloud from books, I ask students, "What is the author telling us?" and then "How does he or she tell us more about this?" or "How does he or she elaborate on this idea?" We begin to make a list and continue adding to it as we study how authors elaborate upon their ideas (see Figure 3.1).

I encourage students to use our list to help them as they try to elaborate in their own writing. Figure 3.2 shows Ashley's writing, in which she tells us what she likes to do (play), where she does it (in her sticker bush fort), who she plays with (Trisha), and what they do when they're there (I sit down, we eat doughnuts). Not only does Ashley elaborate, using the skills she has learned, but she elaborates in a very organized way.

Below is an example of how Heather elaborated in a paragraph about a storm.

THE FRIGHTENING STORM

It was late when the storm happened. The thunder rumbled as the lightning gave a shock. The sea was bouncing off the rocks beside it. You could hear how frightening the storm was. The fog and hail mixed together so it was very hard to see through. The lighthouse was the only light in the storm, but you could barely see it.

TELLING WHAT

"Miss Mattie Perkin's mercantile was stuffed with everything anybody ever could want or need. Coffee beans and crackers were piled in big barrels. Overalls, work boots, and gloves were stacked on low wooden tables. A tall cooler stuffed full of homemade butter, fresh eggs, and Grapette pop . . ."

—*Love, Ruby Lavender,* by Deborah Wiles, p. 8

"He wanted her for his mate but was unable to tell her so because he couldn't make a sound. He swam in circles around her and pumped his neck up and down and made a great show of diving and staying down to prove he could hold his breath longer . . ."

—*The Trumpet of the Swan,* by E. B. White, p. 71

"Paul and his patriot friends wanted to do something to fight the unfair taxes. They formed a new group called the Sons of Liberty. Joseph Warren, Samuel Adams, and John Hancock were its leaders."

—*Paul Revere,* by Jane Sutcliffe, p. 16

"The women were upset. One was clutching her heart. The other was leaning forward and holding a cane with both hands. She walked as if the cane were the only thing holding her up."

—*Cam Jansen: The Mystery of the Stolen Diamonds,* by David A. Adler, p. 13

OTHER BOOKS WITH GOOD EXAMPLES OF TELLING WHAT

• *A Crash, a Roar, and So Much More!,* by Katharine Kenah, p. 13

• *The Pilgrims' First Thanksgiving,* by Ann McGovern, p. 20

• *Red Wolf Country,* by Jonathan London, p. 10

• *Sophie's Masterpiece,* by Eileen Spinelli, p. 11

TELLING HOW

"Some of the Sons wrote clever newspaper articles against the taxes. Paul fought in his own way. He engraved and printed political cartoons making fun of Britain."

—*Paul Revere,* by Jane Sutcliffe, p. 16

"He knew just how to manage on the gusts of wind. He faced full into the wind if he wanted to rise, and let it take him from behind when he wanted speed. He had only to turn his thin edge to the wind, carefully, a little at a time. . . ."

—*Flat Stanley,* by Jeff Brown, p. 29

"Lying on his leafy bed, Jack watched the mother of the baby gorilla groom her small baby. The mother parted his hair and searched through it, picking at his skin now and then.

—*Good Morning, Gorillas,* by Mary Pope Osborne, p. 50

"The place was like a witch's kitchen! All about him black metal pots were boiling and bubbling on huge stoves, and kettles were hissing and pans were sizzling and strange iron machines were clanking and spluttering . . . there were pipes running all over the ceiling and walls."

—Charlie and the Chocolate Factory, by Roald Dahl, p. 88

OTHER BOOKS WITH GOOD EXAMPLES OF TELLING HOW

• *How Georgie Radbourn Saved Baseball,* by David Shannon, p. 26
• *Baby Whale's Journey,* by Jonathan London, p. 13
• *Owls,* by Gail Gibbons, p. 5

TELLING WHEN

"One afternoon late in September, when the air was hazy with smoke from distant forest fires and the sun hung in the sky like an orange volleyball, Ramona was sharpening her pencil as an excuse to look out the window."

–Ramona the Brave, by Beverly Cleary, p. 75

"Next morning when the first light came into the sky and the sparrows stirred in the trees, when the cows rattled their chains and the rooster crowed and the early automobiles went whispering along the road, Wilbur awoke and looked for Charlotte."

–Charlotte's Web, by E. B. White, p. 144

"Of all the rooms at Little School, the one Charley liked best was Mr. Sizemore's. Charley's group went there the last half hour of every Wednesday."

–Did You Carry the Flag Today, Charley?, by Rebecca Caudill, p. 48

OTHER BOOKS WITH GOOD EXAMPLES FOR TELLING WHEN

• *All About Turkeys,* by Jim Arnosky, p. 8
• *Harriet Tubman,* by Catherine Nichols, p.1
• *The Journey of a Turtle,* by Carolyn Scrace

TELLING WHY

"Of all the rooms at Little School, the one Charley liked best was Mr. Sizemore's. . . . In Mr. Sizemore's room the children made things of clay. They colored with crayons. They painted pictures with their fingers on big sheets of paper. They built houses and fences and calf pens with blocks."

—Did You Carry the Flag Today, Charley?, by Rebecca Caudill, pp. 48–49

"Most people—and especially small children—are often quite scared of being out of doors alone in the moonlight. Everything is so deadly quiet, and the shadows are so long and black, and they keep turning into strange shapes that seem to move as you look at them. . . ."

—James and the Giant Peach, by Roald Dahl, p. 31

"Peach slipped an arm under my arm and held my hand. I let him. It felt good to have a hand to hold, even if it belonged to Peach."

—Each Little Bird That Sings, by Deborah Wiles, p. 162

"I am so angry at my mom right now.
She won't let me get my ears pierced.
She's so mean when my dad is around.
She's not acting like the Mom I've always known."

—I, Amber Brown, by Paula Danziger, p. 34

OTHER BOOKS WITH GOOD EXAMPLES OF TELLING WHY
• *Monet,* by Mike Venezia, p. 10

• *Mr. Lincoln's Way,* by Patricia Polacco, p. 4

• *A Picture Book of Rosa Parks,* by David A. Adler, p. 15

TELLING WHERE

"Next morning, when his parents were not looking, Louis took off into the air. He flew northeast. When he came to the Yellowstone River, he followed it to the Sweet Grass country. When he saw a town beneath him, he landed . . ."

—The Trumpet of the Swan, by E. B. White, p. 54

"He was talking with Mrs. Lambchop one afternoon when her favorite ring fell from her finger. The ring rolled across the sidewalk and down between the bars of the grating that covered a deep, dark shaft. Being flat could also be very helpful, Stanley found."

—Flat Stanley, by Jeff Brown, p. 10

"Jack and Annie started through the cloud forest. They walked around huge trees draped with moss. They pushed past tall shrubs and leafy plants.

—Good Morning, Gorillas, by Mary Pope Osborne, p. 13

OTHER BOOKS WITH GOOD EXAMPLES OF TELLING WHERE
• *Charlie Anderson,* by Barbara Abercrombie, pp. 19–20

• *The Quilt Story,* by Tony Johnston and Tomie dePaola, p. 8

MODELS FROM LITERATURE

CAUSE-EFFECT/TELLING WHAT HAPPENED NEXT

"There was a dull explosion as the egg broke, and then a horrible smell. Fern screamed. Avery jumped to his feet. The air was filled with terrible gases and smells from the rotten egg. Templeton, who had been resting in his home, scuttled away into the barn."

— *Charlotte's Web,* by E. B. White, p. 72

"Billy shut his eyes and *popped* the last piece of worm into his mouth, chewed, gagged, clapped his hands over his mouth, gulped! gulped! toppled backward off the orange crate."

— *How to Eat Fried Worms,* by Thomas Rockwell, p. 25

ANOTHER BOOK WITH A GOOD EXAMPLE OF TELLING WHAT HAPPENED NEXT

• *Barefoot: Escape on the Underground Railroad,* by Pamela Duncan Edwards, p. 14

Telling Stories First

Students love to tell stories. Every day my students come into the classroom, bubbling over with things they want to tell me: "I got new shoes." "My dog got lost over the weekend." "You know what happened last night?" I always tell them, "That's a great writing topic." I remember to tap into these stories during writing workshop. Young students can learn to elaborate, if we teach them to "tell their stories first." This oral component is so important. Many young children need to talk and need to hear their stories, before they can believe they have something to write.

So I model this when I write in front of students. I talk my stories first, telling students the details I want to write before I ever pick up the pen. I also encourage students to tell their stories first to friends. Always, with first graders, we turn to a partner and "tell" what we are going to write. Adena turns to Reilly and tells him about going on a ferry ride and buying a stuffed seal. Linnae tells Jordan about a cat who needs a name and is asking the reader for advice. And Taylor tells Bobby about his baseball game over the weekend.

This sharing of stories helps students realize they do have something to write, and also have details to add. Partners serve as helpers when students are "stuck" and would like to tell more but can't think of anything. Often, partners remember something from the told story and can suggest adding that detail. They also can help by asking questions, which may lead to *telling more.*

TELLING STORIES FIRST

Some of the best mini-lessons include teacher modeling. When students see teachers really work to make their ideas come to life in a story, they learn a lot about the strategies being taught, as well as the writing process itself.

Introduce the Purpose of the Lesson

If I want students to see the power in telling their stories first, I need to show them how this works. I begin my lesson by telling students this:

"Today I'm going to write about something I saw last night when I got home. I think I would like to talk my story first, so I can get my ideas going in my head. Is that okay?" Students are usually quite supportive.

Modeling

I begin, "Last night I got home and I saw this pretty large spider web in my doorway. In the middle I saw a spider and it was about the size of a pencil eraser. It was just sitting in the middle of the web. I knew I would have to duck to get into the door so I wouldn't disturb the web. I didn't want to wreck it because I know it probably took a long time for the spider to build it. I didn't see any flies in the web and I wondered if the spider had caught anything yet. Anyway, when I came out of my door this morning, it was still there, and so was the spider. The web kind of glistened in the morning light. I wonder if it will still be there when I get home tonight."

Students listen with great interest. When I stop, they actually have some questions for me. What color was the spider? How big was the web? I tell students, "You know, it really helped me to tell my story first. It got my mind focused on my story and now I really know what I want to write. I know I have a lot to say."

I proceed to write my story in front of students, adding to some of my oral ideas.

Here's the story I modeled writing for my students.

After writing my story, students compare my "told" story with my written one. They agree I included much of what I had told in my writing. As students go off to write, I encourage them to find partners. Each partner is to tell his or her story first, adding as much detail as possible. When both students have shared, they may begin writing.

Students Give It a Try

As I circle the room, it is very clear that students have stories to tell. Like dominoes falling, students find places to write, and begin. . . .

After drafting time, we gather to share some writing and to reflect on what we learned today. I begin with a question. "Did telling your stories help you when you went to write?"

A flurry of hands go up. Jarred shares, "It really helped me to tell my story about seeing the different colored leaves because then I remembered some of it when I was writing."

"Great! Anyone else?"

Miya adds, "When I told all the things I knew about horses, it gave me some ideas to write down when I wanted to add some details."

And Robbie says, "I got to tell about my trip with my dad and grandpa and then I had ideas to write down."

"Wow!" I say. " It sounds like telling your stories was helpful. Remember, you can do this any time you think it might give you some ideas."

◆

MINI-LESSON

TELLING BEFORE WRITING— A STUDENT CO-TEACHES

Students can be wonderful co-teachers during mini-lessons, and co-teaching can be a very powerful learning experience for them. Not only does the student who is co-teaching learn a ton of new things, the other students see that they can do this too.

Introduce the Purpose of the Lesson

I begin by reminding students about our last lesson: We told our stories before we wrote them. I refer to my story about the spider that came to live in my doorway, which is now on a chart in the room. We revisit some of our reflections about how telling our stories helped us write. I actually recorded student comments in my journal, so I read those again today. "Many of you feel that telling your stories is a good way to gather ideas for writing."

Modeling With a Student

I start, "Today, I have asked Haley to tell her story to us. I asked her earlier this morning so she could think about what she would like to write about. Have you had a chance to think of a topic, Haley?"

Haley nods, as she comes to the front of the room. "I am going to write about the rainbow I saw yesterday."

I encourage Haley. "That's a great topic. What would you like to tell us about the rainbow?"

Haley begins, and as she does, I take notes on sticky pads. "Well, yesterday I saw a rainbow in the sky and it was really pretty. It had red and yellow and purple in it."

Haley stalls, and so I ask, "Can you tell more by telling where? Where were you when you saw the rainbow?"

"I was on the playground at recess," she continues. The sky was really gray with clouds and then this rainbow just stood out in the sky. It was like a present from God."

While Haley is talking, I am taking notes, recording some key phrases. I make sure I record her last comment accurately.

"Wow, Haley. That is an incredible story about the rainbow you saw. I love your description—let me look here [I look down at my notes]—that 'it was like a present from God.' That is such a poetic sentence and such a great ending to a story."

I share with Haley, and the rest of the class, the notes I took while Haley told her story. I offer them to Haley, as reminders of all she wants to say when she goes to write. Again, I encourage students to tell their story to a friend before they write.

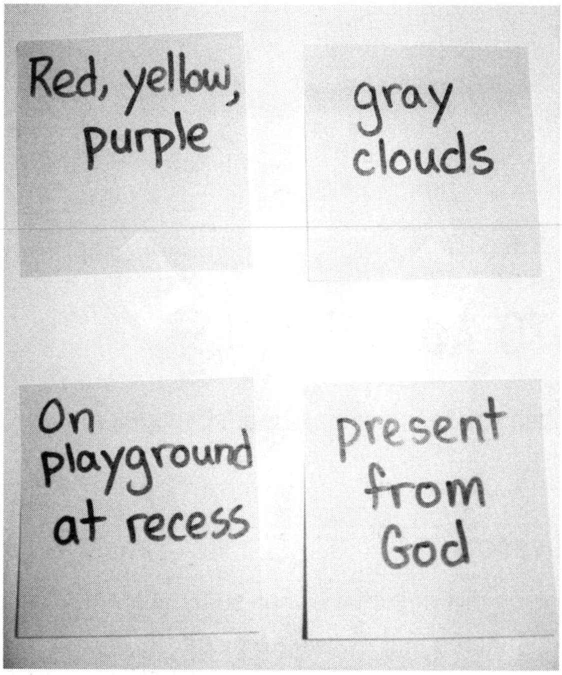

Figure 3.3
The notes I created for Haley to help her elaborate.

Adding Details

With beginning writers, often the details come in their pictures. Take Alex, for example. He writes, "We saw a pig yesterday."

Alex has written only one sentence but look at what else he has told us. His picture shows a black and white pig with a curly tail (see Figure 3.4). He seems to be looking at us. Alex has labeled the pig "Oreo." In Chapter 7 I will show how a teacher might confer with Alex to help him add more details to his writing.

Figure 3.4
Alex's drawing and writing about a pig.

MINI-LESSON

USING PICTURES TO ADD DETAILS

I always say, you need to do three things when you teach writing: model, model, and model some more.

Introduce the Purpose of the Lesson

I begin lessons on adding details by focusing on drawn pictures. For some students, this is the springboard for their writing. I tell students that drawing a picture is a great prewrite. It gives us ideas and details we might not think about otherwise.

Before beginning to draw today, I tell students I want to write about a walk I took in the old marsh by my home. I talk my story, telling students about everything I saw: ducks diving for fish, a brilliant pink/orange sunset, cattails all around, green reeds sticking up from the water, an old bridge.

Modeling

I begin by drawing each of these things I described, using color to emphasize detail. Then, for my young students (first graders), I write this:

> Last night I went for a walk by the old marsh. It was a beautiful autumn night. A pink and orange sunset spilled on the water. Cattails stood tall all around me. Ducks dove in the water, looking for fish, I think. It was a peaceful moment.

As I write, I refer back to the details of my picture, modeling for students how to take what I see, and turn it into another sentence. I encourage them to do the same. I tell them, "As you draw your picture, add as many details as you can. Use color to help you remember. When you think you have a detailed picture, begin writing. Keep looking at your picture to help you add details."

For second graders (and some first graders), I either write quickly in front of students, or come the next day with a piece already written and ready to share. I might post my writing and read it to the class, or simply read from my journal. This piece has more detail and the language is more sophisticated, because I expect more from older students. If we expect a lot, we need to model a lot.

> Last night was a beautiful autumn night – the kind of night that beckons you to take a walk . . . and so I did—down to the Kirkland wetlands, the marsh.
>
> I walked along the bridge and stopped at a sight that made me catch my breath. Sunset spilled upon the lake, creating a pink-orange mirror. Clouds, like outstretched arms, spread across the sky. Cattails guarded a marshy spot where three ducks dove for dinner. One duck glided across the water, jutting his head—forward, backward, forward, backward. The ducks were in a world of their own—peaceful, quiet, serene. I was their visitor.

We talk about the details I shared—what I saw on my walk. We return to our How Do Authors Elaborate? Chart (see Figure 3.1). Students share about the ways I elaborated.

Serena begins, "You told *when* by saying, 'Last night.' And you also told *where* when you mentioned the Kirkland wetlands."

Mason adds, "You also told *what* you saw—the cattails and the sunset and what the ducks were doing."

I prod students, "How about my sentence about the clouds? Who can read that?"

Jessica says, "You tell us they spread across the sky like outstretched arms. That's a simile."

"You're right. What kind of telling did I write there?"

Bobby jumps in, "You told how . . . how the clouds spread across the sky . . . like outstretched arms."

"Yes. These are all details I remember from telling my story first, then drawing it, and finally looking back at my drawing to help me remember. You can do this too. As you go off to write today, sketch out your story. Use your drawing to help you remember the details you want to add."

MINI-LESSON

ELABORATING ON IDEAS IN SHARED WRITING

After my modeling, I'm ready to have students work with me on elaborating ideas during shared writing. I often connect learning in reading workshop with learning in writing workshop. So when students read about pandas in *Scholastic News* and other resources, I suggested pandas as a topic for shared writing.

Students decide they would like to create a class book about pandas. I suggest to students, "We probably need to review what we've learned and take notes." I record facts recalled by students on separate 9" x 12" sheets of paper that hang along the board.

Live in China	Eat bamboo	Black and white	Baby pandas tiny

After taking notes, we look at the pages to decide on a logical order. I place another 9" x 12" paper under each of the originals, and we begin writing, elaborating as we go. I start, "We have made 'black and white' our first page. How can we make that a complete sentence?"

Tatum says, "Pandas are black and white animals."

Miya adds, "We should say they are 'large black and white animals.'"

I record Tatum and Miya's ideas as a sentence and then ask, "Okay, how can we tell more about this?"

Josh answers, "We can say, 'They have thick fur.'"

"We also can tell how much they weigh," adds Tyler.

"Great ideas. Does anyone remember what we read about that?"

Adena gets one of our panda books and tells us, "Pandas weigh 200–300 pounds."

Pandas

by
Ms. Sloan's
First & Second
Graders

What are pandas?

Pandas are large black and white animals. They have thick fur and weigh 200-300 pounds. 1

Where do pandas live?

Wild pandas live only in forests in China. Some live in zoos. They are an endangered species. 2

What do pandas eat?

Pandas eat bamboo. Bamboo looks like trees but it's actually a kind of grass. 3

Figure 3.5
First four pages of our book Pandas.

"Okay, Can we add these details? How shall we say it?"

Adena says, "Pandas are large black and white animals. They have thick fur and weigh 200–300 pounds.

"I love it," I respond as I record ideas. "Look—we started with *Pandas are black and white*. We elaborated with interesting details and now we have:

Pandas are large black and white animals. They have thick fur and weigh 200–300 pounds.

We work through each page. *Pandas live in China* becomes:

Wild pandas live only in forests of China. Some live in zoos. They are an endangered species.

Pandas eat bamboo becomes:

Pandas eat bamboo. Bamboo looks like trees. But it's actually a kind of grass.

By asking questions and talking through ideas, students are able to elaborate upon each idea, making eight pages for our book. We add a dedication and About the Author pages, and we have our finished product, ready to illustrate and then enjoy in the classroom (see Figure 3.5).

Final Thoughts

Every teacher who has ever taught a science concept or a topic in social studies, and then asked students to take their notes and use them to write a report or essay, knows one of the real difficulties for students is elaborating on the few sentences they have about a particular point. This kind of shared writing lesson can give students support as they learn to elaborate on ideas.

If we don't begin early—teaching students how to tell more after making a statement—we aren't preparing them for what they will need to do in later grades. However, if we take the time to teach different strategies for telling more—like telling what, where, when, how, why, or talking through stories first, or using drawings/sketches to gather ideas—we give students a "trunk of tricks" to use when they write.

CHAPTER 4

*U*SING OBSERVATIONS TO ELABORATE

It is a soft spring day. Green leaves cover the trees, and flowers bloom everywhere one looks. There is a warm wind. As I walk my students back from music to our own room, we stop to enjoy a garden of yellow and red tulips. Students surround the garden, taking in all there is to see. With urgency, Mackenzie says, "Look! There's a butterfly."

We gather around and observe an orange butterfly with black and red markings. It lands on a flower, its wings still. It sits like a statue, just for a moment, and then, as a soft breeze sweeps across the flowers, the butterfly's wings flit, and then flutter, and the butterfly dances its way through the air in a zigzag pattern.

As we watch the butterfly fly away, I tell students, "We just experienced a moment in time."

Discovering Moments in Time

There are moments all around us, everywhere. These moments are experienced, and often observed. If we stop to pay attention, usually these moments can make incredible stories and poems. In their book *A Note Slipped Under the Door: Teaching From Poems We Love* (2000), Nick Flynn and Shirley McPhillips address four kinds of moments:

- An everyday moment
- An observed moment
- A remembered moment
- A moment that happened only once

Certainly, my butterfly moment was an observed moment, and although I can certainly say it will happen again in my lifetime, it was what I call *a once in a while* moment.

Sometimes moments overlap, slip into one another. For instance, a remembered

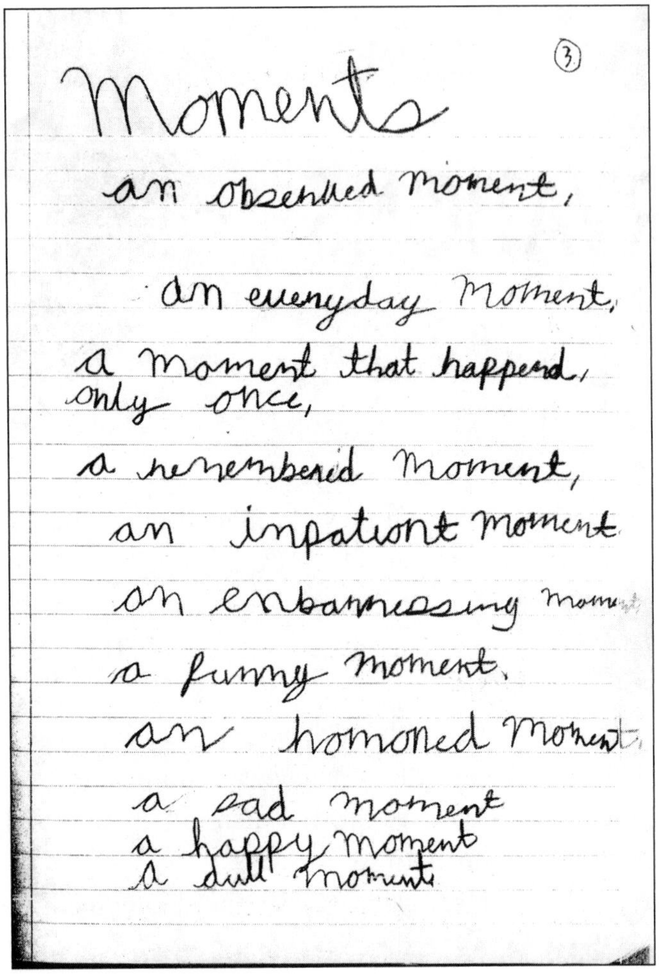

Figure 4.1
Katherine's list of possible moments to write about.

moment can also be a moment that happened only once. An everyday moment is often an observed moment.

These four moments mentioned by Flynn and McPhillips are helpful, but certainly not exhaustive. There are variations and permutations of these poetic occasions (see Figure 4.1).

Our job as teachers is to help young writers discover their own moments and learn to tell those moments in slow motion. In other words, we need to teach students to slow down the moment for the reader in one of the following ways:

1. Describe the moment by telling what you see, hear, taste, smell, or touch (observations).

2. Tell what you think, tell how you feel, or tell what someone said.

3. Use language as a vehicle for stretching the moment. (This strategy can be used for numbers 1 and 2, but I include it separately to make it stand out to students.)

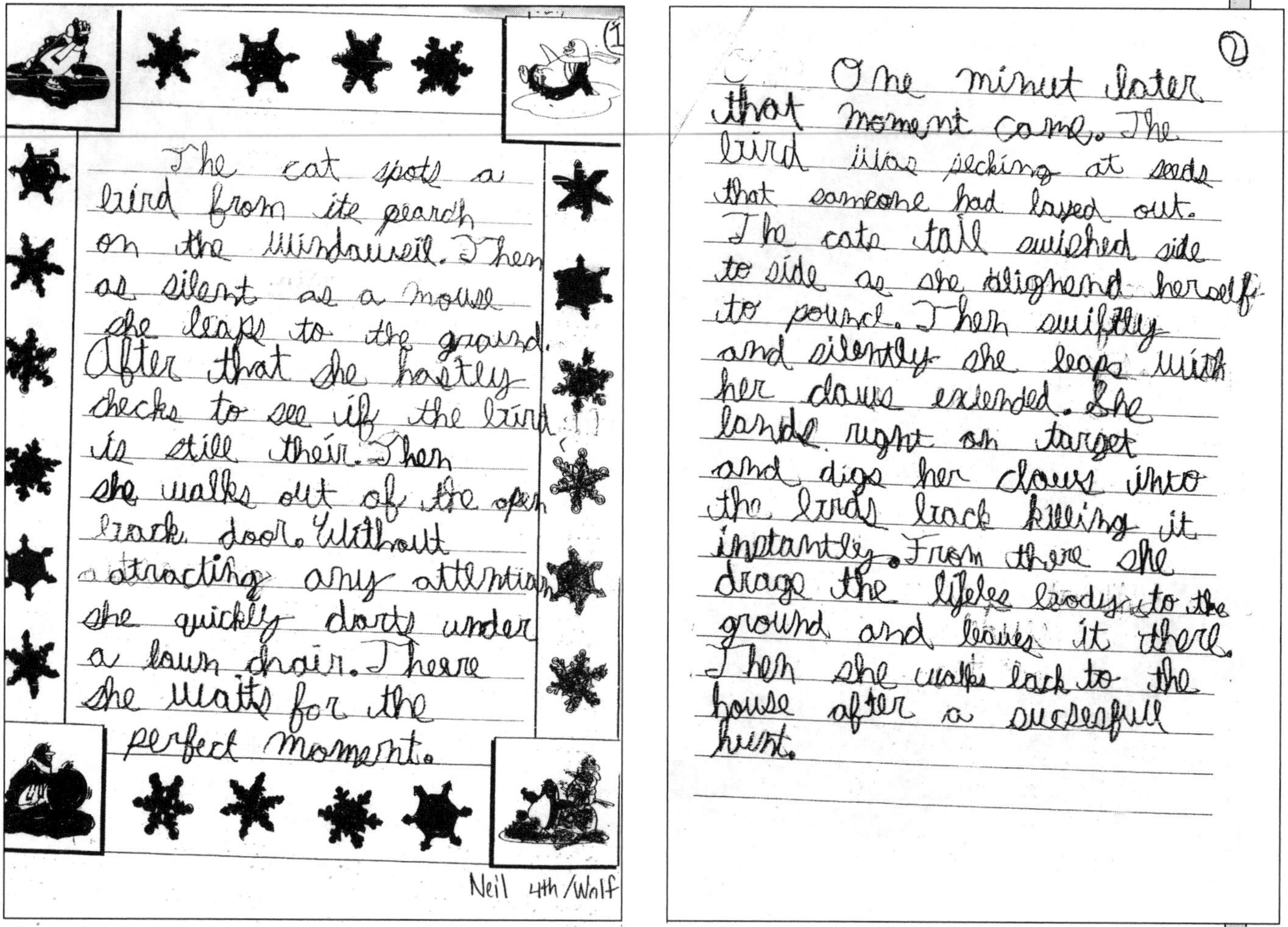

The cat spots a bird from its perch on the windowsill. Then as silent as a mouse she leaps to the ground. After that she hastily checks to see if the bird is still their. Then she walks out of the open back door. Without attracting any attention she quickly darts under a lawn chair. There she waits for the perfect moment.

Neil 4th /Wolf

One minute later that moment came. The bird was pecking at seeds that someone had layed out. The cats tail swished side to side as she alighned herself to pounce. Then swiftly and silently she leaps with her claws extended. She lands right on target and digs her claws into the birds back killing it instantly. From there she drags the lifeles body to the ground and leaves it there. Then she walks back to the house after a succesfull hunt.

Figure 4.2
Neil slows down the moment he observed.

DISCOVERING MOMENTS IN STORIES

In Chapter 2, I wrote about narrowing the topic. In terms of this chapter, that really means discovering the real moment in a story. I used a baseball game as an example. Writing about the whole game would feel a little like a bed-to-bed story. "In the first inning . . . and in the second inning . . ." and so forth. Instead, I picked the moment in the game where the real story happens: the ninth inning. That is where I started because that is where the story begins.

We also need to teach children to discover moments around them that are not part of a bigger story. Some of these might include a butterfly landing on a flower and flitting through a garden or a wind storm that comes upon you suddenly. A moment might include, as it did for Brenda Wolf's student Neil (see Figure 4.2), a pet eyeing its prey and all that leads into the kill. We need to teach our students to be observant, to pay attention to the world around them.

Describing the Moment

The senses are powerful tools. If a writer can fully describe the sights, sounds, smells, tastes, and touches during a particular moment, the reader will be transported to its center, experiencing the moment as if he or she were there.

We need to give our students plenty of opportunities to "stop and smell the flowers," time to stop and talk about what they see or hear or smell. I often do this as we walk out to recess or lunch, or walk back from music or P.E. Our building has outdoor hallways so I have plenty of opportunities to say, "Wow! Look at those clouds. They're so dark, but look at the way the sun is shining down through them." Or, "My goodness, do you feel that breeze? It just swept across my face. It feels like spring today. And smell the air! The flowers are so fragrant. They smell like cherries today." Or, "Come look at this spider on its web. It is hanging by a delicate strand. And the web is glistening in the morning sunshine." When I start with comments like these, students chime in, and soon they are the ones capturing the moment first, telling me what they see, hear, feel, smell, or taste.

CONNECTING TO TEXT To illustrate the technique of using one's senses to describe a setting, character, or moment, I turn to our favorite books. Patricia Polacco is a master of elaboration. In *My Ol' Man*, Polacco begins her story by thinking back to when she was a young girl. She talks about her summers in Michigan and describes how she and her brother wait for their dad to come home each evening. She describes everything she sees: her house, her grandmother watering the plants and admiring her crepe-paper parrots, the mailman avoiding a neighbor's dog, and finally herself and her brother on the front porch.

After reading the first page, I stop and tell students, "Wow! I feel like I'm right there in the scene, waiting with them for their father to come home. How many of you feel that way too?" Many hands go up. "Why do you suppose we feel that way? What does the author do to make us feel part of her story?"

Tatum answers, "She tells us what's going on."

Robbie adds, "It's like she's telling us everything she sees."

"Like what?" I ask.

"Like the dog chasing the postman," says Johnny.

"And their grandma watering her plants in the window, and her parrots," adds Miya.

Tyler raises his hand and shares, "She says, 'There's our house on Middle Street.'"

I comment, "You are right. Patricia Polacco tells us all the things she sees. She describes the scene by telling us about everything and everyone who is there. Authors want us to feel like we are in the story, so they often tell us what a character sees, hears, feels, smells, or tastes, so we can experience that too. They add details as a way to stretch out the moment, make it last a little longer, as we read."

On a subsequent day, I read from Kate DiCamillo's *Because of Winn-Dixie*. DiCamillo describes one of the characters, Miss Franny Block, as she arrives at a party.

> She was wearing a pretty green dress that was all shiny and shimmery. And she had on high-heeled shoes that made her wobble back and forth when she walked. Even when she was standing still, she kind of swayed, like she was standing on a boat. (p. 145)

I stop reading, put the book on my lap, and say, "There it is again. The author slows down the moment by describing someone or something. In this case, who is the author describing?"

Several students yell out, "Franny Block."

I agree, "Yes. What does she tell us?"

Alex says, "She tells us she wobbles on her high-heeled shoes."

I nod. "Yes. What else does she say about her wobbling?"

"That she looks like she's standing on a boat," says Jordan.

I ask students to close their eyes and see the picture in their heads. "Do you see her wobbling, like she's standing on a boat?" Students nod. "Can you see what she's wearing?"

Jordan shouts out, "A green dress, and it shines and shimmers."

I add, "Oh yes, it looks like a fancy dress to me."

Students open their eyes. I explain that authors use words to help us make pictures in our heads. In this case, DiCamillo describes what India Opal sees as Franny Block arrives to the party. She stops time for us. She uses words to paint a picture so we can experience the moment, just as if we were there.

As our days continue, I point out passages in books where authors slow down the moment by telling what they sense. I try to include all the senses so that students can see authors elaborate by describing what they see, hear, smell, taste, and feel. For instance, I move from texts that describe only sights, to those that describe sights and sounds, as well as the other senses. It doesn't take long before students are pointing out these passages to me and to their classmates.

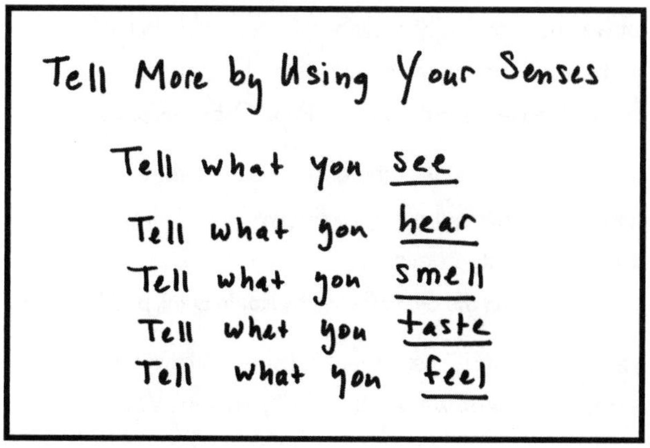

While taking the part of baby frog in *Animal Babies in Ponds and Rivers*, Jennifer Schofield elaborates by using sights and sounds. She describes a frog's eye color and size, as well as the noises it makes.

In *Miss Rumphius*, Barbara Cooney elaborates by telling what the character

Tell More by Using Your Senses

Tell what you <u>see</u>
Tell what you <u>hear</u>
Tell what you <u>smell</u>
Tell what you <u>taste</u>
Tell what you <u>feel</u>

Figure 4.3
Our class-created chart about using our senses to tell more.

feels and smells. Miss Rumphius steps inside a conservatory and feels the warmth and wetness of the air as it wraps around her. She smells sweet jasmine.

I don't share long descriptions with students. I want them to know that elaborating by telling what one senses can be just one or two additional lines. They can do this in their own writing, too. Together students and I create a chart (see Figure 4.3).

Examples are best chosen from books your students are familiar with, such as read-alouds, class novels, or independent reading. Here are some models.

Using the Senses to Elaborate

MODELS FROM

L I T E R A T U R E

CHAPTER BOOKS

"He didn't look . . . good. He was big, but skinny; you could see his ribs. And there were bald patches all over him, places where he didn't have any fur at all. Mostly, he looked like a big piece of old brown carpet that had been left out in the rain."

— *Because of Winn-Dixie*, by Kate DiCamillo, p. 11

"The skin of the peach was very beautiful—a rich buttery yellow with patches of brilliant pink and red."

— *James and the Giant Peach*, by Roald Dahl, p. 26

". . . There was a rug on the floor . . . , a light recessed in the ceiling and another in the wall next to a table. There were bookshelves; on one shelf an electric clock hummed quietly to itself. A book lay open on the table, with a chair in front of it . . . ."

— *Mrs. Frisby and the Rats of NIMH*, by Robert C. O'Brien, p. 98

"The autumn days grew shorter, Lurvy brought the squashes and pumpkins in from the garden and piled them on the barn floor . . . The maples and birches turned bright colors and the wind shook them and they dropped their leaves one by one to the ground . . . ."

— *Charlotte's Web*, by E. B. White, p. 173

"The scene was a like a nightmare. The tent was hot and stuffy. A dozen injured soldiers lay on small cots. Some called for food. Others begged for water or just moaned."

—*Civil War on Sunday* (Magic Tree House Series), by Mary Pope Osborne, p. 26

"The tunnel was damp and murky, and all around him there was the curious bittersweet smell of fresh peach. The floor was soggy under his knees, the walls were wet and sticky, and peach juice was dripping from the ceiling . . . . It tasted delicious."

— *James and the Giant Peach*, by Roald Dahl, p. 34

"About three feet in length, and more than a foot tall, Marty the Fisher had short, brown fur and small, round eyes almost blank with emotion. His legs were stubby but powerful. With his sharp claws he could climb trees and leap about branches as nimbly as a squirrel."

— *Ereth's Birthday*, by Avi, p. 11

"Finally we're worn out and turn the car for home. I rest my head on my arms, folded on the frame of the open front-seat passenger window. The sun is warm on my cheek, and the wind blows through my hair and fills the car with the sweet scent of freshly mown hay."

— The Green Dog, **by Suzanne Fisher Staples, pp. 94–95**

"Of all the rooms at Little School, the one Charley liked best was Mr. Sizemore's. . . . In Mr. Sizemore's room the children made things of clay. They colored with crayons. They painted pictures with their fingers on big sheets of paper. They built houses and fences and calf pens with blocks."

— Did You Carry the Flag Today, Charley?, **by Rebecca Caudill, pp. 48–49**

PICTURE BOOKS

• *Harvesting Hope: The Story of Cesar Chavez,* by Kathleen Krull, p. 9

• *Owl Moon,* by Jane Yolen, p. 11

• *The Royal Bee,* by Frances Park and Ginger Park, p. 13

• *The Seashore Book,* by Charlotte Zolotow, p. 7

• *William's Doll,* by Charlotte Zolotow, p. 12

◆

MINI-LESSON

MODELED WRITING–
USING ONE'S SENSES TO ELABORATE

After sharing many book examples of using one's senses to elaborate, I model this strategy for my students. It is March, so I begin writing a leprechaun story. I show students my first two sentences.

One fine day I was walking along a path in the woods.
Suddenly I spied a little man.

I ask, "What do you think of my story so far?"
Students are polite. They like my first few words and they think I used an interesting word (*spied*). However, when I ask them, "Have I elaborated very much about the woods or the little man?" they say no.

I reread my sentences and then I begin, "Hey, we have been working on elaborating by telling what we see, hear, feel, taste, or smell. I could do that here. After telling, 'One fine day I was walking along a path in the woods,' I could tell what I heard or saw." I revise by adding some details.

One fine day I was walking along a path in the woods. I saw big leafy trees overhead. The leaves were green, yellow, and orange. I felt a soft, cool breeze sweep across my cheek. All of a sudden I heard a tapping sound.

I ask students, "How do you like that?"

Jessica says, "It's much more interesting because you tell what you see, hear, and feel."

"Yes," I continue. "I like it better too. It tells my readers more about the moment. Let me try doing the same thing with my second sentence, "'Suddenly, I spied a little man.'" Again, I revise.

Suddenly, I spied a little man. He had on a green button-up coat and a three-cornered hat. He was singing a sweet song, and I could hear him humming too.

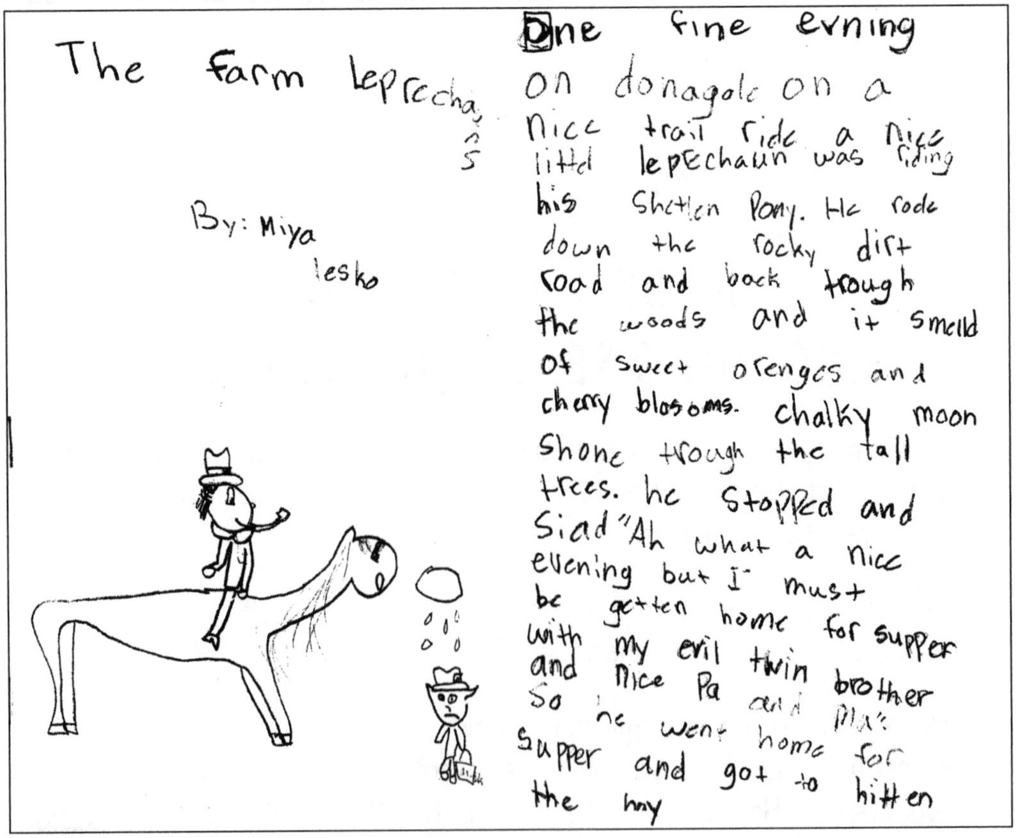

Figure 4.4
Miya elaborates by telling what she senses.

"What do you think?" I ask.

"That's way better," says Josh. You tell what he is wearing (what you see) and what you hear."

I wrap up now. "You know, it's not that hard to elaborate by telling about what you see or hear, or smell, taste, or feel. You just have to put yourself in that moment and tell more about it."

I encourage students to think about telling more by telling what they see, hear, smell, taste, or feel. I refer them to our chart and remind them to look at it for ideas as they work to elaborate. I am looking for experimentation. I want students to try this. I don't expect them to master the technique. I am reminded of Vicki Spandel and Rick Stiggins's *Goals for Primary Writers*. "Teach ourselves to identify moments of . . . details . . ." (1997). That is what I want: "moments of details."

Student Samples

> We drove the thunderbird. It is red.
>
> From "The Hunting Trip," by Robbie, first grade

> My favorite place is my room. . . . My room looks like a sky, which is on my wall. And my bed has flowers on it. And I just have two lights: one—my lamp, two—my switch light. If you came to my house, it's going to be messy. Clothes are on the floor and my toys are everywhere.
>
> —Haley, second grade

> One fine evening in Donegal, on a nice trail ride, a nice little leprechaun was riding his Shetland pony. He rode down the rocky dirt road and back through the woods and it smelled of sweet oranges and cherry blossoms. A chalky moon shone through the tall trees.
>
> —From "The Farm Leprechaun," by Miya, third grade

> I love walking through the woods. The birds are chirping and sometimes you can hear the wind as it blows through the trees.
>
> —Jarred, third grade

> Dear Mrs. Sloan,
>
> We had a wonderful time [at the beach]. I could taste saltwater. I saw a sea star. It was spikey. I also saw a sun star. It was slimy. I heard sounds of waves crashing against the sand.
>
> Love, Tatum [second grade]

Slowing Down the Moment: Tell What Someone Says, Thinks, or Feels

Another way to capture the moment is to stop and tell what you or the character is thinking, feeling, or saying. This stretches the moment, and the reader gets a chance to reflect more deeply about the character, event, or setting.

TELL WHAT SOMEONE SAYS

Stopping to tell what someone says to another person, character, or themselves is a lovely way to extend a moment.

CONNECTING TO TEXT In *Brave Irene*, William Steig elaborates on the predicament of his main character by telling what she says. Irene is caught in a terrible snowstorm. She twists her ankle and lies stranded. She blames her problem on the wind

Telling What Someone Says

MODELS FROM LITERATURE

"Hidden in a hole in the wall of the princess's bedroom, the mouse listened with all his heart. The sound of the king's music made Despereaux's soul grow large and light inside of him. 'Oh,' he said, 'it sounds like heaven. It smells like honey.'"

—*Tale of Despereaux*, by Kate DiCamillo, p. 27

"Susan gasped. Ramona twisted the owl as hard as she could until it looked like nothing but an old paper bag scribbled with crayon. Without meaning to, Ramona had done a terrible thing.

   'Mrs. Griggs!' cried Susan. 'Ramona scrunched my owl!'

   'Tattletale.' Ramona threw the twisted bag on the floor."

—*Ramona the Brave*, by Beverly Cleary, pp. 54–55

"Templeton, of course, was miserable over the loss of his beloved egg. But he couldn't resist boasting. 'It pays to save things,' he said in his surly voice. 'A rat never knows when something is going to come in handy. I never throw anything away.'"

—*Charlotte's Web*, by E. B. White, p. 74

"After a few days Karen complains that I'm hogging the dog.

   'He's not just your dog,' she says.

   'He is!' I say with more feeling than necessary. 'I take care of him. I'm the one who wanted a dog!'

   'He belongs to the entire family,' my mother says. . .'"

—*The Green Dog*, by Suzanne Fisher Staples, pp. 44–45

and shouts out for the wind to stay quiet. She tells the wind that it has caused enough damage, spoiling her very important errand.

I ask students, "How did Steig slow down the moment? How did he keep you there for a minute?"

Tyler answers, "He tells you what Irene says when she's stuck."

"Yes," I agree. William Steig keeps us in this moment by showing us what Irene says to the wind. I infer that she is mad at the wind. She says it's spoiling everything. Her words stretch out the moment and thus make us feel we are there. When we hear Irene's actual words, we understand her frustration and disappointment."

MINI-LESSON

MODELED WRITING– TELL WHAT SOMEONE SAYS

I decide to write a quick piece in front of students. I tell my story first and then write (see Figure 4.5).

As I write, I think aloud. At the point where I add dialogue, I actually say, "Hmm, I think this would be a great point to slow down the moment. I could tell what Julia asked me: 'Auntie! Would you help me with my puzzle?' Now I can tell what I said back: 'Sure,' I said." I continue talking as I write. "Then she said, 'You put the outside together. I'll put the inside together.'" I want students to see that adding dialogue is a conscious choice a writer makes.

I tell students, "The dialogue is what makes this moment so special, so I want to include it." I encourage students to think about ways they might include some dialogue to stretch their moments.

Student Sample

WHERE'S YOUR TREASURE?

A long time ago there was a leprechaun and a girl (me) with her dog. I wanted to find a leprechaun and then I spotted one and I rushed to him with my dog.

I grabbed the leprechaun and I stuck him in a can. Well, he squirmed and squiggled and pushed and pulled. But I didn't give up.

barbecue
✗Julia-puzzle

Dad → emergency room

I just love going to see my nieces Julia & Katie! My niece, Julia <u>loves</u> puzzles. She's very good at putting them together. She's just 4 yrs old. Last night she said, "Auntie! Would you help me with my puzzle?" "Sure," I said. We sat down and began. →

She said, "Auntie - you put the outside together." I'll put the inside together." We set to work. I had a hard time - but not Julia! She was a wiz! We slowly put Strawberry Shortcake together!

Figure 4.5
A piece about helping my niece Julia build a puzzle, which I wrote as a model for my students.

I yelled, "Give me your treasure." He gave me a strange look. "Show me where your treasure is and I'm not letting you go until I have it."

So he directed me straight to the rainbow. I marched and marched and finally it was above my head. I blew up a balloon and flew up and grabbed the gold in a sack but I peeked in first. . . . ."Mountains of gold! Thank you. I love it."

So I went home and I was rich as a queen.

—Emma, second grade

TELL WHAT SOMEONE THINKS OR FEELS

Telling what someone feels or thinks is a great way to stretch time and keep one's reader in the moment.

■► **CONNECTING TO TEXT** Our current read-aloud, *Poppy*, has lots of examples of elaborating on ideas. I don't have to read far today to find an excerpt that shows this technique of *telling how someone feels or what they think*.

Avi introduces his character Poppy. Poppy is being watched and desperately needs to find a place to hide in Dimwood Forest.

> *It did not take long before an exhausted Poppy had to stop. Her sides ached. She was hot and cold all at once. Her heart felt as though it would break out through her ribs. Gasping for breath, she crept beneath a leaf, then peered about.* (p. 83)

Telling What Someone Thinks or Feels

MODELS FROM

LITERATURE

"The boys and girls one by one ran their fingers the length of the snake skin to hear it crackle like fire—all but Charley. At that moment Charley almost wished he didn't have the hat. He longed to feel the snake's skin and to hear it crackle."
— *Did You Carry the Flag Today, Charley?*, by Rebecca Caudill, p. 73

"It did look pretty. It looked so pretty that it made my heart feel funny, all swollen and full, and I wished desperately that I knew where my mama was so she could come to the party, too."
— *Because of Winn-Dixie*, by Kate DiCamillo, p. 145

"That cancer was like bugs in a tree: one day you don't see them at all and the next it seems like they're everywhere, eating the leaves and the fruit. And it won't work to find them and squish them one by one. You have to do something drastic."
— *Ida B*, by Katherine Hannigan, p. 66

"Just then the answer came to him, rounding the corner. Pete! And who should be with Pete but Amber Faye Gorbish, Pete's classmate—and more important to the story—Delilah's owner. Just the thought of Delilah made Howie's heart sink, but he refused to give in to sentiment."
— *It Came From Beneath the Bed*, by James Howe, p. 65

"She wondered what it would be like to spend her days in one of the upstairs classrooms. Anything would be better than the first grade. What if I don't go back into Room One? she thought. What if I hide in the girls' bathroom until school is out?"
— *Ramona the Brave*, by Beverly Cleary, pp. 87–88

I stop and ask students, "Avi is describing Poppy's journey through Dimwood Forest. How does he slow down the moment here?"

Immediately, a few hands go up. Miya shares, "Well, he tells you her heart was going to break."

Josh adds, "And he says her sides ache and she was hot and cold all at once."

"She was gasping for breath," says Jarred.

I nudge students to define what this is. "Yes, you are right. He told us all of these things. Is Poppy saying these things, feeling them, or thinking them?"

Many students chime in, "She is feeling them."

"Right. She feels hot and cold. She feels her sides aching. Avi could have chosen not to share these things, but it makes the story more interesting to know how Poppy feels."

Students agree that the story is better with these details. I say, "Good authors do this. They slow down the moment by telling you how or what a character feels during the story. This is something you can do in both fiction and in stories about yourself. If the stories are about you, you can tell how and what you are feeling.

MINI-LESSON

SHARED WRITING— TELL WHAT SOMEONE THINKS OR FEELS

I wrote down the first two sentences of my original leprechaun story.

> One fine day I was walking along a path in the woods. I spied a little man.

I reminded students how I was able to elaborate by adding what I saw and heard.

> One fine day I was walking along a path in the woods. I saw big leafy trees overhead. The leaves were green, yellow, and orange. I felt a soft, cool breeze sweep across my cheek. All of a sudden I heard a tapping sound.
> Suddenly, I spied a little man. He had on a green button-up coat and a three-cornered hat. He was singing a sweet song, and I could hear him humming too.

I suggest to students, "You know, one way to elaborate is by using your senses, telling what you see or hear, feel, taste, or smell. Another way is to tell what someone says (adding dialogue). A third way to elaborate is by telling what a character is thinking or feeling. I think it would be fun to take my original sentences and try to elaborate by telling what I am feeling and thinking. Would you like to help me?"

Students agree to help, and we set to work.

One fine day I was walking along a path in the woods.

"Who has an idea about something I am thinking or feeling?"

Tatum suggests, "You can add, 'I was feeling a little scared because it was dark and I didn't know my way.'"

I praise Tatum. "That is wonderful."

"Now you can add, 'I thought I should be getting home because my mom would not want me out after dark,'" says Lauren.

"Wow," I say. "You are really good at this!"

I write down their ideas.

One fine day I was walking along a path in the woods. I was feeling a little scared because it was dark and I didn't know my way. I thought I should be getting home because my mom would not want me out after dark.

"Let's work on the second sentence. How can we tell more about this? Remember—something I'm feeling or thinking."

I spied a little man.

Joelle suggests, "How about, 'I thought he might be a leprechaun and I got pretty excited because I might get his gold'?"

"Great!" I add Joelle's sentence.

Quickly, Christian adds, "My heart started to beat faster when I thought of this."

Now we have:

One fine day I was walking along a path in the woods. I was feeling a little scared because it was dark and I didn't know my way. I thought I should be getting home because my mom would not want me out after dark.

I spied a little man. I thought he might be a leprechaun and I got pretty excited because I might get his gold. My heart started to beat faster when I thought of this.

"Wow, I am very excited. I think this story tells so much more than my two original sentences. See how telling what someone is feeling or thinking can really add to a story?"

Students agree. I make sure they know that an author can do all of these things: *tell what someone senses*, *tell what someone says*, *tell what someone thinks*, and *tell what someone feels*.

Again, we make a chart to help students, and I encourage them to try one or some of these in the stories they write.

How Authors Tell More

Tell what someone senses

Tell what someone says

Tell what someone thinks

Tell what someone feels

Figure 4.6
Our chart about ways to tell more.

Samples of Students Telling More in Their Writing

How would you like to hear about my pet guppies? I bet you do! I got my guppies from Santa Claus. They were so cute! They are a boy and a girl. We got three more but they died. I was so sad. I cried all night. I was lonely, even though I had my other fish. Goldie and Dragon are going to have babies in a month. I think so, but today Dragon died. It broke my heart to see Dragon die.

—From "My Guppies," by Jessica, second grade

My favorite place is in my backyard. I have a rock in my backyard. I like to sit on that rock and look up and see my great grandma and grandpa just staring at me. It makes me feel warm inside. I can feel the wind rushing past me. My heart beats fast enough. I can feel every person in my family just listening. I enjoy my rock.

—Emma, second grade

Stretching the Moment With Literary Elements

Sometimes authors stretch a moment by using literary elements such as simile, metaphor, onomatopoeia, or alliteration. They don't *have* to add this bit of lovely language to their text, but by doing so they both enrich and elaborate upon a moment. I teach and use these terms with young students. A first or second grader can understand what alliteration or simile is if you embed it into every lesson possible.

CONNECTING TO TEXT I like to start with simple yet eloquent examples, so who better to begin with than Jane Yolen? I read *Owl Moon*, stopping to celebrate the places where she stretches the moment by using a simile. Yolen describes the moon over a clearing in the woods. She compares its color to "milk in a cereal bowl."

We savor the language. As I read the passage again, I invite students to listen to the way Jane Yolen stretches the moment.

"How does the author describe the snow?" I ask.

Isabella answers, "She says, 'it's whiter than the milk in a cereal bowl.'"

"Yes, she's comparing snow to milk. How are they alike?"

Taylor says, "They're both white."

Megan reading a picture book to students.

"Yes. That's called a simile and it's an element of language that can help an author stretch a moment."

Joelle adds, "And it sounds good too!'

I agree, "Yes it does."

We reread *Owl Moon* and discover similes we missed. Yolen compares the trees to statues, the sound of the forest to the quiet of a dream, and when describing the great owl, she says he is like a soundless shadow. We discuss how similes are a beautiful way of telling more.

As we continue reading books, I show students how authors also use metaphor, alliteration, and onomatopoeia to stretch a moment. Some of the texts I use are listed below.

How Authors Use Literary Elements

MODELS FROM

LITERATURE

CHAPTER BOOKS

"The next day was foggy. Everything on the farm was dripping wet. The grass looked like a magic carpet. The asparagus patch looked like a silver forest."

— *Charlotte's Web*, by E. B. White, p. 7

"The king adjusted his heavy gold crown. He cleared his throat. He strummed his guitar and started to sing a song about stardust. The song was as sweet as light shining through a stained-glass window, as captivating as the story in a book.

— *The Tale of Despereaux*, by Kate DiCamillo, p. 29

PICTURE BOOKS

- *All the Places to Love,* by Patricia MacLachlan, pp. 10, 12, 14, 18, 21
- *Brave Irene,* by William Steig, pp. 12, 18, 24, 27
- *The Eyes of Gray Wolf,* by Jonathan London, pp. 6, 10, 20
- *Pumpkin Circle: The Story of a Garden,* by George Levenson, pp. 4, 5, 6, 11, 17, 18
- *Red Wolf Country,* by Jonathan London, pp. 14, 7, 10, 13, 15
- *The Seashore Book,* by Charlotte Zolotow, pp. 10, 12, 14, 18

MODELED WRITING– USING LITERARY ELEMENTS TO STRETCH THE MOMENT

I tell students that I have an idea for my writing today. I was inspired by something I saw as I was driving to school.

> This morning I saw a cat run across the road right in front of my car. It zipped past me. I wondered, "Where are you going?" and "Where have you been? Were you up to no good?" The cat moved quickly and soon he was out of sight. I will keep wondering about that cat all day.

After writing, I reread my piece and ask students, "Do you think there is anywhere in my piece where I could stretch this moment using a simile or a metaphor?" I start reading again: "This morning I saw a cat run across the road right in front of my car."

Jarred asks, "What color was the cat?"

I answer, "It was black. Hey, I've got an idea. I could say . . . 'I saw a cat black as . . . ' I ask students, "What is really black?"

Robbie answers, "Midnight."

"That's great. I could say, ' . . . I saw a cat black as midnight, run across the road in front of my car.' I like that. You helped me add a simile to elaborate."

I keep reading my story and stop when I get to: "It zipped past me."

I ask students for more help. "I like this part. I bet I could add another simile by comparing the cat to something else that goes really fast. Hmm . . . 'It zipped past me like . . . .'

Miya raises her hand. "Like lightning," she suggests.

"Oh, I like that. *It zipped past me, fast as lightning.* That's a great simile, and it tells more about how the cat was moving."

As students set out to write, I remind them of all the ways authors elaborate: telling what someone senses, feels, thinks, says; and stretching with language. I encourage them to think of similes that might work to tell more about a character or event in their stories. I don't require them to use this sophisticated language in their writing, but as students become more comfortable, many will give it a try. Then they might help teach the next mini-lesson.

Student Samples of Elaborating Using Literary Elements

One fine spring day I was walking along to the pond. I had my yellow raincoat on me. I saw a turtle waddling slowly to the pond too. Then the clouds began to spill rain, rain that was dropping like leaves falling gently to the ground.

—Serena, first grade

Figure 4.7
Evan, a first grader, elaborates using a simile.

My favorite place to go in the whole universe is to my Aunt Marilyn and Uncle Jim's house in North Bend. The Snoqualmie River is in my aunt and uncle's backyard. In their yard they have beautiful glittering daisies, poppies, and my favorite, roses. It smells so, so fresh, like a summer breeze in the mountains. When I am there it makes me feel as free as a wild honking goose flying south.

—Taryn, third grade

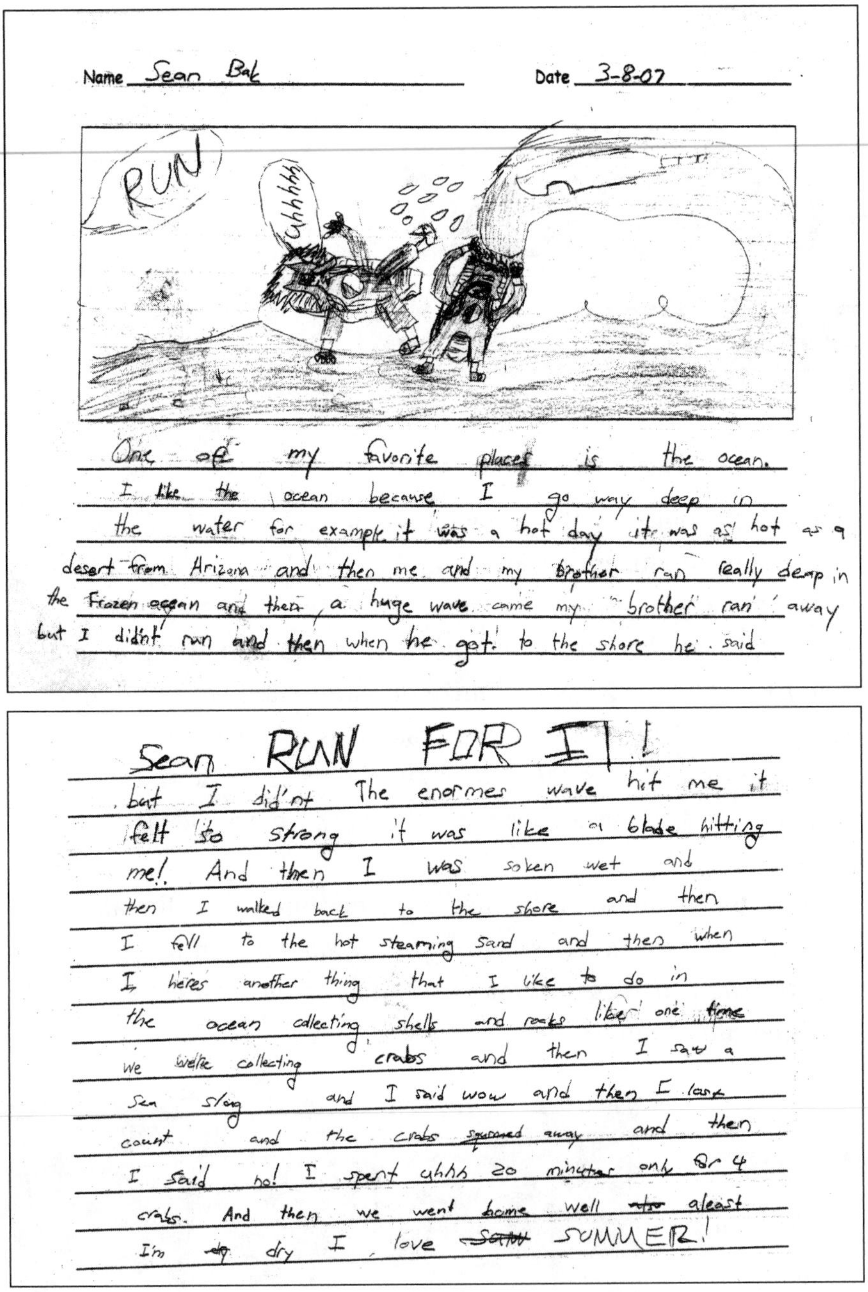

Figure 4.8
Sean, a second grader, elaborates using examples and a simile.

Final Thoughts

Defining elaboration as "telling more" simplifies writing for students. Having them practice elaborating by telling what they see or hear, or telling what they feel or think, will help students expand upon their ideas, making the stories they write more interesting for their readers. You may also find the form on page 134 a useful tool for encouraging students to tell more.

CHAPTER 5

USING QUESTIONS TO ELABORATE

Children have questions about everything—what gorillas eat, how a shadow is made, and why Pluto is no longer considered a planet by United States scientists. They also wonder about people, real ones as well as characters from books. *Why did Harriet Tubman risk her life to save others? How does Avi's Poppy conjure up enough courage to fight Mr. Ocax? Would I make the same choice to stand up to my enemies?* I teach students to ask questions as they read. This makes them more thoughtful readers. As we read from *Turtles Take Their Time*, by Allan Fowler, I encourage students to ask questions. I record these questions, and now we have ideas for research right in front of us.

Likewise, I teach students to ask questions as they write because this will make them more thoughtful writers. *Does this make sense? Is there something missing? Will my reader know why the character acted in this way? Did I connect these two ideas? Did I tell enough so my reader understands?*

Writers' Questions

In previous chapters I wrote about elaboration in terms of telling more. Writers tell more by telling what, telling how, telling where, telling why, telling when, and telling who. These statements can be turned around to make questions. This chapter is going to extend the idea of telling more by introducing mini-lessons to include asking questions to elaborate.

Figure 5.1
A class-created chart about writers' questions.

USING QUESTION CARDS
TO HELP STUDENTS ELABORATE

I begin my writing workshop lesson by talking about two puppies who visited our classroom yesterday. They are Chris's puppies and he is glad I chose this topic. I begin by remembering aloud what the pups looked like, what they did, and what Chris shared about them. Then I announce, "I think I will write about the puppies today."

I start by asking students to point out where I will begin. Carly comes up and points to the top left side of the paper and indicates I write across the paper and come back. This is an easy way to include instruction on left to right and spacing for young students who need it. (This step is obviously skipped for students who are older and do not need this instruction.)

I begin my first sentence.

Yesterday Chris brought in two puppies.

"Let me reread this to see if it makes sense." I reread my sentence. "That sounds a little boring. How could I describe the puppies to make my sentence more interesting?"

Many students raise their hands. I choose Alex. "Small," he says.

"Yes." I insert *small* right before *puppies*. "That tells more about them. How else could I describe the pups?"

Joelle answers, "One was black and one was brown."

"Great," I agree. I elaborate by adding that sentence next.

"Let me go on." Next I add:

Chris will need to take care of them.

I go back and reread everything I have written. "Hmm, I could ask myself a question right now." I hold up a card that has the word *HOW* written on it. "I could ask myself, 'How? How will Chris take care of the puppies?'"

Students chime in, "He will need to feed them."

As I write down their words, I say, "Yes, and I could ask myself WHY." I hold up a WHY card. "Why does Chris need to feed them?"

"So they will grow strong," says Lauren. I add her sentence.

I continue writing.

Chris will also need to walk them and play with them.

Using a question card to prompt children to tell more.

Again, I hold up the WHY card. "Why does he need to walk them and play with them?"

Chris adds, "So they will get exercise."

Yes. I add on to my sentence.

Chris will also need to walk them and play with them so they get exercise.

I finish up with a last sentence.

Puppies are very fun pets, but they can be hard work.

My finished piece:

Yesterday Chris brought in two small puppies. One was black and one was brown. Chris will need to take care of them. He will need to feed them so they will grow strong. He will also need to walk them and play with them so they get exercise. Puppies are very fun, but they can be hard work.

In addition to the question word cards I use during lessons, I have students make their own question cards to put in their writing folders. These serve as reminders to ask questions as they write.

WHAT ELSE DO YOU WANT TO KNOW?

In this lesson, I am able to *show* students how important it is to add details to their writing.

I gather students and begin, "Today I am going to write about something I did over the weekend." I write my sentence on the chart.

I went for a walk yesterday.

"Okay, I'm done." A moment passes.

Tyler asks, "Is that all you're going to write?"

I answer, "Well, it's all I was thinking about writing. What else do you want to know? What else could I tell you about my walk that would be interesting?"

Johnny asks, "What was the weather like?"

I begin to talk as I write. "It was very sunny, and there was a cool breeze. Okay, I'm done."

Tatum asks, "Where did you go?"

I reply, "Oh, where did I go? I write my sentence as I answer out loud. "I went down to the path by Lake Washington. Okay, I'm done."

Bobby raises his hand. "Did you see anything?"

I get excited, "Yes, I saw a bunch of ducks swimming in the water. They were diving for food and zigzagging back and forth as they swam." I add my new sentences to my story. "Oh, and I also saw a whole flock of geese flying overhead in a V shape. It was very cool." Again, I add my sentence. Now I have:

I went for a walk yesterday. I went down to the path by Lake Washington. It was very sunny, and there was a cool breeze. I saw a bunch of ducks swimming in the water. They were diving for food and zigzagging back and forth as they swam. I also saw a whole flock of geese flying overhead in a V shape. It was cool.

For some first graders I may stop here. For older students I continue.

I reread what I have and ask, "Is there anything else you want to know?

Taylor asks, "Who did you go with?"

"My sister went with me," I say. Then I say, "You know, I think this sentence would fit better up here after *I went for a walk yesterday.*" I insert a caret symbol and teach students that writers often insert ideas later.

"How about one more question for me? What else do you want to know about my walk?"

Jenna says, "How did you feel when you were there?"

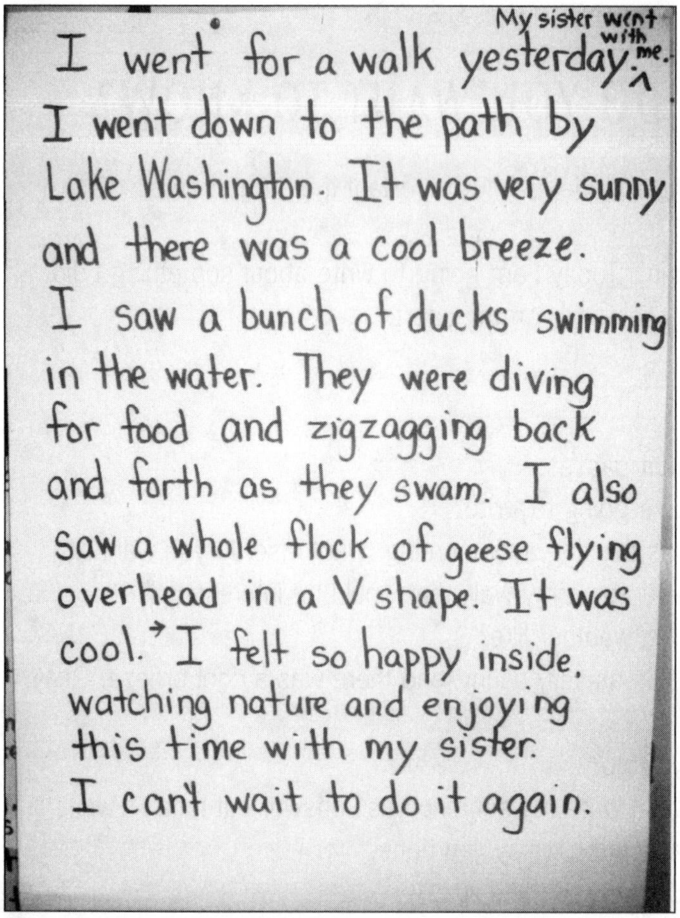

Figure 5.2
The piece I used to model how to elaborate using questions.

"Oh, Jenna, this is a perfect way to end my piece." As I talk, I write: "I felt so happy inside, watching nature and enjoying this time with my sister. I can't wait to do it again."

I reread my story. "Boys and girls, I really have to thank you today. When I first wrote "I went for a walk yesterday," I thought that was all I had to say, but you helped me see that I left my readers with so many unanswered questions. When you asked me all your great questions like 'Where did you go?' and 'How did you feel when you were there?' you gave me ideas for elaborating."

I continue, "Sometimes I feel the same way about your writing. You leave me with lots of unanswered questions. Today as you write, think about the questions on our board, or take out your question cards from your writing folder. When you think you are done writing, ask yourself some of these questions and see if they inspire you to tell more."

USING QUESTIONS TO ORGANIZE A CLASS BOOK DURING SHARED WRITING

As students experiment with different ways to organize their writing, I like to introduce them to books that are organized in a variety of ways. One way some nonfiction authors organize a text is by asking a question at the top of a page and then answering that question either at the bottom of the page or on the next few pages. For example, in Christopher Nicholas's *Spiders!,* the author begins with "What is a spider?" He continues on subsequent pages with questions such as "What do spiders eat?" "Why do spiders spin webs?" and "How do spiders protect themselves?" After Nicholas asks the question, he answers it with text and pictures, as well as other text features such as bold print, labels, close-ups, and charts. When Nicholas answers the question about a spider's home, he explains by telling the many places spiders can be found around the world, such as forests, caves, the tropics, and more.

The pictures show different kinds of spiders (labeled) in different habitats. There is a chart labeled "Spiders Live In" with bulleted items listed. There are close-ups and bold print.

Another way authors use questions is by providing text about a topic at the top of a page, and asking a question at the bottom, perhaps to be answered on the next page. In *Animal Babies in Grasslands*, for example, Jennifer Schofield gives clues alongside the picture of a baby animal and then asks the question *Who is my mommy?* The subsequent page answers the question and adds some details about what the baby and mommy animal do together.

I share many books with students to show them how authors organize their ideas using questions. Once they are comfortable with this format, I provide an opportunity for students to give it a try.

We begin with a shared writing experience. I ask students to name some animals they would like to read and write about. Students have many ideas, but finally settle on owls.

I ask, "What are some burning questions you have about owls?"

Jesse answers, "Where do they live?" I record Jesse's question on a chart.

Miya adds, "We should first ask, 'What are owls?'" I record Miya's question on a different chart.

"What else?" I prod.

"What do they eat?" says Adena.

"How do they get around?" adds Jordan.

"This is a great beginning," I say. "Why don't we also make a chart with the question, 'Is there anything unusual or special about owls?'"

So now we have several charts, each with a question, and we can begin reading. We choose Gail Gibbons's *Owls* to start. As we continue reading and learning about owls, we realize we have also learned a lot about owls through our fiction read-aloud, *Poppy*, by Avi. We discuss the fact that even fiction authors have to research certain things so that their stories are believable. Avi had to know that owls eat mice, but don't eat porcupines, or he could not have written his story the way he did.

We now record on our charts what we have learned.

| WHAT ARE OWLS?

• nocturnal
• birds with feathers
• many kinds
• different sizes | WHERE DO OWLS LIVE?

• hollow trees in the forest
• tree stumps
• ground
• abandoned birds' nests | WHAT ARE SOME OTHER SPECIAL THINGS ABOUT OWLS?

• Their heads can twist almost completely around.
• They have great hearing—use it for hunting.
• They can see great distances.
• Bones are light—full of air. |
| HOW DO OWLS MOVE?

• soar
• move powerful wings
• swoop down to catch prey | WHAT DO OWLS EAT?

• birds, snakes, insects, and rodents like mice and squirrels | |

Figure 5.3
Our question chart about owls.

Like our panda book in Chapter 3, we take the information we have and try to put it into a text with clear and complete sentences. When we are ready, I suggest to students that we start with the first question on the chart: What are owls?

"Okay, let's take this question and try to answer it using our notes. What are owls?" I write this question on a clean chart. "How can we begin?"

Joelle suggests, "Owls are wonderful animals."

Jessica continues, "They have feathers and great big wings."

I keep writing. "What else? What should we say about them being nocturnal?"

Isabella adds, "They are nocturnal."

"Yes. What does that mean?"

Isabella continues, "It means they are awake at night and sleep during the day."
"Okay. What else do we have in our notes?" I ask.

Josh raises his hand. "There are 140 different kinds of owls."

I prod, "Like what?"

Jarred adds, "Like the great horned owl, the spotted owl, and the snowy owl.

Adena quickly adds, "The smallest owl is the elf owl."

I ask, "How small is the elf owl?"

Mackenzie looks up the data in one of our books and answers, "It is five inches long. And the largest owl is the great gray owl. It is thirty-three inches long."

As I quickly record student ideas, I say, "Wow, we have some data to back up our ideas. That's great. Let's reread what we have for our first page."

WHAT ARE OWLS?

Owls are wonderful animals. They have feathers and great big wings. They are nocturnal. That means they are awake at night and sleep during the day. There are 140 different kinds of owls like the great horned owl, the spotted owl, and the snowy owl. The smallest owl is the elf owl. It is 5 inches long. The largest owl is the great gray owl. It is 33 inches long.

"Wow. We may want to split this up into two pages. We will have to decide that."

We move to the second page, going through the same process; then the third, fourth, and fifth pages. We take our notes and turn them into complete sentences so that we have a book with lots of interesting details.

We publish the book, illustrating each page, and it becomes a model for students as they set out to write their own animal books organized by questions.

MINI-LESSON

USING QUESTIONS TO ORGANIZE THE WRITING OF INDIVIDUAL BOOKS

With a class model, students are now ready to research their own animals and organize individual books using questions. I display many animal books for students to browse. Once they pick a book, I ask them to read about their animal and take notes as they read. I give them a graphic organizer to help them organize their thoughts (see Figure 5.4) and pages 135 and 136 in the Appendix.

What are _____ ?	Where do _____ live?
What do _____ eat?	How do _____ move?
What are some special things about _____ ?	What are unusual things about _____ ?

Figure 5.4
A graphic organizer for helping students write about an animal.

Students take notes as they read, and then organize their notes into complete sentences to make an animal book. They use a question at the top of each page as a way to organize their thoughts. I've included a sample of a student's note sheet in Figure 5.5 and the student's book in Figure 5.6.

Name: Tatum	Animal: Penguins
What are penguins? thick coat Shiny feathers Black white yellow and some red	Where do penguins live? South pole Sonwing places
What do penguins eat? fish Krill	How do penguins move? waddle Slide Swim
egg called rookery build nests hole nest babys cute	Big Emperor little fairy or littleBlu Emperor No nest

Figure 5.5
Tatum's note sheet.

Figure 5.6
Tatum's book.

penguins

What are penguins?
penguins are black and white.
They have a thick coat so they
can stay warm. They also have
shiny feathers.

Where do penguins live?
penguins live in the South pole
and snowing places.

What do penguins eat?
penguins eat fish and krill. Krill
is a kind of fish.

How do penguins move?
penguins waddle, swim and slide. But mostly
penguins waddle thow. waddling is when you rock
to side to side.

instring things about penguins.

penguins build nests. The eggs are called rooke
The bigest penguin is the EMPEROR penguin. And
the littlest penguin is called little blue or fairy.
The Emeror penguin dose not mak nests.
The fairy is up to your nee.

pages and Titles.

what are penguins? 1-2
where do penguins live? 3-4
what do penguins eat? 5-6
How do penguins move? 7-8
instring things about penguins. 9-10

USING THEIR WORK TO HELP STUDENTS ASK QUESTIONS AND ELABORATE

Some of the most powerful mini-lessons I have taught involve the use of student work and student help. Chase, a beginning second grader, wrote about seasons during writing workshop (see Figure 5.7).

I praise Chase for including all of the seasons and writing great ideas about each one. I tell him that I would love to hear more about each season. After our conference, I ask Chase if he would like to help teach my next mini-lesson, where students would help give him ideas for elaborating on his writing. Chase agrees.

We agree that Chase's lead sentence: "Seasons are fun" should stay as it is. I write Chase's second, third, and fourth sentences onto the first column of our chart.

We begin with his second sentence: "Winter is a season." Students know they are helping Chase elaborate by asking questions that would help him think to add some details. We ask the question "What kind of season?" Chase answers, "Winter is a really great season." I record this onto the second column (see Figure 5.8). Then we move to sentence number three: "It snows in winter."

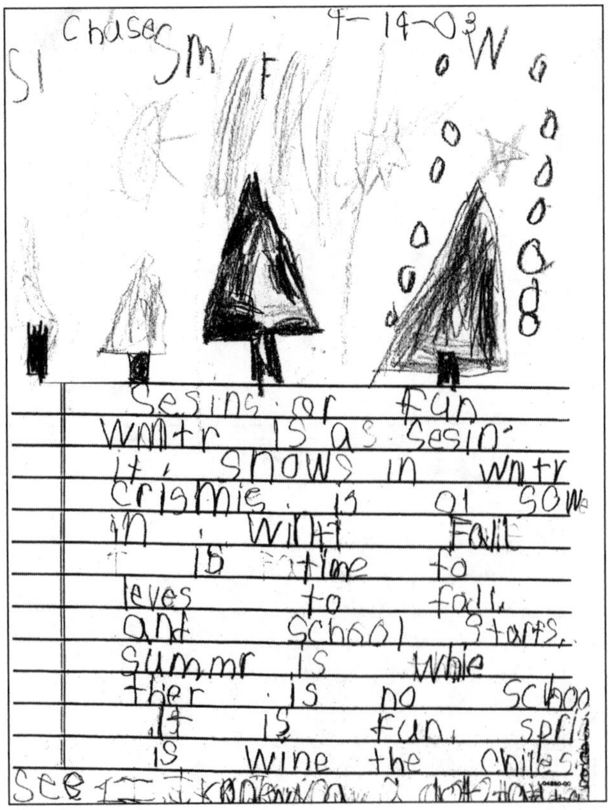

One student asks, "What can you do in the winter?"

Chase answers, and I record his sentences onto the second row and second column (see Figure 5.9).

"Wow, Chase! Already, I'm seeing how asking you some questions really helps you tell more. Let's do another sentence." Chase reads: "Christmas is also in winter." Students immediately ask him, "What do you do at Christmas?" As Chase answers and students chime in with some thoughts, I record ideas (see Figure 5.10).

Last, we tackle Chase's

Figure 5.7
Here is Chase's original piece.

ORIGINAL SENTENCE	ELABORATION
Winter is a season.	Winter is a <u>really</u> <u>great</u> season.
It snows in winter.	
Christmas is also in winter.	
Fall is a time for leaves to fall.	

Figure 5.8
The beginning of our elaboration chart.

ORIGINAL SENTENCE	ELABORATION
Winter is a season.	Winter is a <u>really</u> <u>great</u> season.
It snows in winter.	It snows in winter. You can make snowmen and have snowball fights. The snow is fun to watch while it softly comes down.
Christmas is also in winter.	
Fall is a time for leaves to fall.	

Figure 5.9
The class helps elaborate on another one of Chase's sentences.

ORIGINAL SENTENCE	ELABORATION
Winter is a season.	Winter is a <u>really great</u> season.
It snows in winter.	It snows in winter. You can make snowmen and have snowball fights. The snow is fun to watch while it softly comes down.
Christmas is also in winter.	Christmas is also in winter. You give presents and you see colorful lights twinkling off the snow.
Fall is a time for leaves to fall.	

Figure 5.10
The chart is almost completed.

ORIGINAL SENTENCE	ELABORATION
Winter is a season.	Winter is a <u>really</u> great season.
It snows in winter.	It snows in winter. You can make snowmen and have snowball fights. The snow is fun to watch while it softly comes down.
Christmas is also in winter.	Christmas is also in winter. You give presents and you see colorful lights twinkling off the snow.
Fall is a time for leaves to fall.	Fall is a time for colorful leaves to drop off the trees, flutter down and rest on the ground.

Figure 5.11
The finished chart.

sentence about fall. After Chase reads, "Fall is a time for leaves to fall," students ask, "What kind of leaves? What color? Where do they fall?"

Chase answers and I write. Again, students help Chase with their ideas (see Figure 5.11).

This lesson is obviously great for Chase, but it also is helpful to other students as they work to ask questions to help them elaborate on their ideas. They see how it works for a real student piece. Chase can now take his story and continue to ask himself questions as he elaborates on the rest of his ideas. We eventually have a publishing conference and Chase shares his finished book with the class.

Chase's revised version:

SEASONS ARE FUN.

Winter is a really great season. It snows in winter with little white flakes of snow going down very slowly. You can make snowmen and make snow angels. Christmas is also in winter. You give presents and see colorful lights on Christmas trees and roofs.

Fall is a time for colorful leaves to flutter down and rest on the ground. School starts and you learn a lot. The air gets crisp and it gets chillier.

Summer is when there is no school and it's super hot! You go swimming in the pool and jump into the pool. Families go on vacation. We go to Cannon Beach. There's lots to see in Cannon Beach.

Spring is when the chill is in the air. Flowers grow out of the earth. Bees and other animals come out of hibernation.

Seasons are fun.

—by Chase, second grade

◆

MINI-LESSON

FATTENING UP THE SKELETON STORY BY USING QUESTIONS TO REVISE

Whether it is the first grader who writes only one sentence and can tell you nothing else, or the third grader who has written a paragraph, but leaves out all of the possibly interesting details that would fill in the gaps, students often write stories that are "all bones." They need assistance in seeing that their writing can be made better by "plumping it up" or adding details.

I ask students to write about something they did over spring break. Students share their ideas and then set off to write. I purposely do not model first. At the end of our writing workshop, I collect the students' writing.

The next day I gather students and tell them that I read their pieces from yesterday and would like to share my piece about my spring break. I have purposely written with very few details.

> During spring break I went to the zoo. I saw lots of animals. We walked around for two hours. We had lunch and rested under a big tree. It was a fun day.

I ask students, "What do you think of my writing?"

They say they like my topic, but then Taylor adds, "I wish you told more."

I ask, "What do you mean?"

"Well, I have some questions."

I invite Taylor to come up to the front with me.

I read my piece to Taylor again and I ask him, "What questions do you have for me?"

Taylor says, "What animals did you see and did you have a favorite?" He adds, "And were they doing anything special?"

I say, "Oh, I see I didn't say anything about that." I record Taylor's questions on a chart. "What else?"

"Who did you go to the zoo with?"

I answer, "Okay, what else?"

Taylor says, "How did you feel about going to the zoo? Were you tired walking around for so long? What did you have for lunch?"

I record all of Taylor's questions. Then I set out to revise in front of students so they can see how I tackle this. I reread my piece along with Taylor's questions. I think aloud as I draw arrows and squeeze ideas in between other sentences. I make changes and add more.

> During spring break I went to the zoo. It was a hot day—a perfect zoo day! We saw lots of animals: lions, hippos, giraffes, penguins, and many more.
>
> My favorite animals were the elephants. They were playing in the yard. The baby was following her mom around and throwing her trunk in the air. One elephant made a loud trumpeting sound. The zoo keeper finally called them in to eat. One by one they followed him inside.
>
> After two hours we were exhausted. We sat down and ate a picnic lunch under a big shady tree. It was peaceful. You could

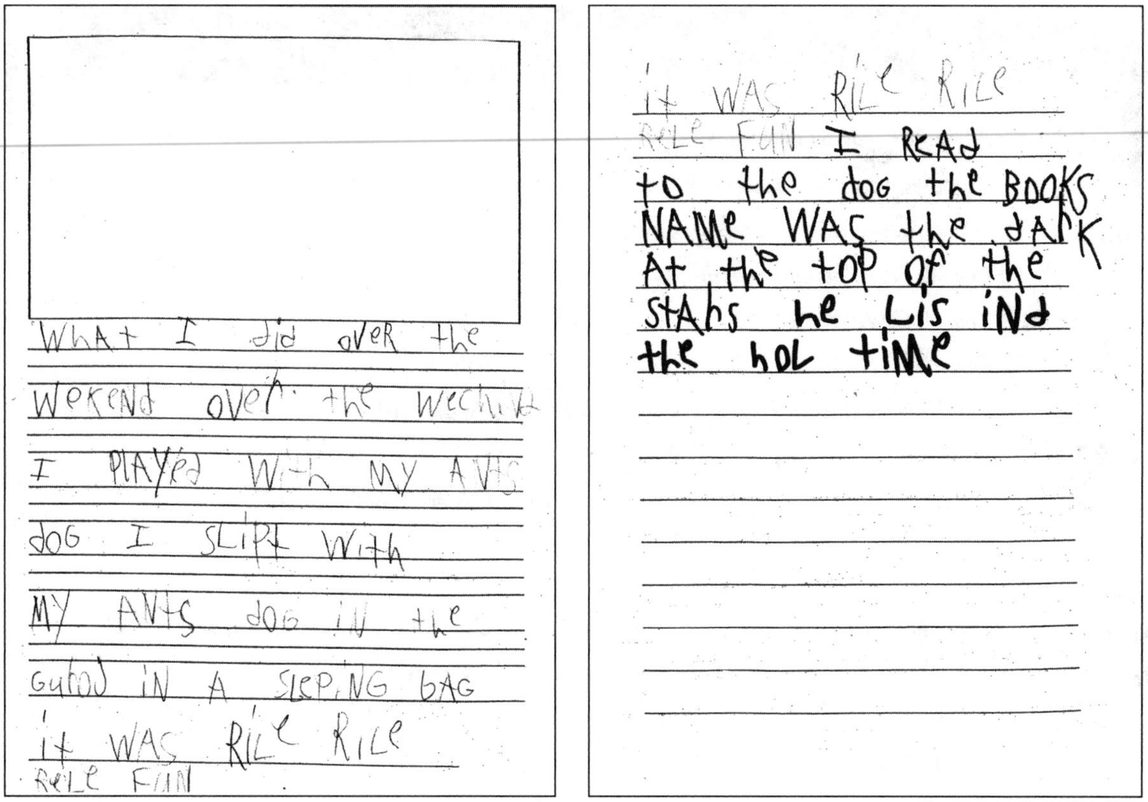

Figure 5.12
Robbie's writing before and after revision.

hear birds chirping, and little kids were playing and laughing. It
was the perfect spring day!

I reread my finished piece and ask students which one they like better—the first
one or this one. All agree that this story has more details and leaves the reader with
a better sense of my day at the zoo. I tell students that my first piece was like a
skeleton—all bones. When I elaborated, with the help of Taylor's questions, I added
flesh and muscle to my skeleton.

Now I address the student pieces from yesterday. I tell students, "You know,
when I read your stories about your spring breaks, I was left with questions just like
you were when you read my story. Taylor really helped me when he asked all these
questions [I point to my chart]. I was able to revise my story, adding lots of interesting details. Today, I would like you to find a partner and read your stories to each
other. Ask your partner at least three questions his or her writing left you wondering
about. Write them down and give them to your partner. Then each of you should
work to revise your story for details. Fatten them up. Add some flesh and muscles to
your skeleton stories!" For younger students I might ask them to ask two questions.
For older students, I might require that they ask four or five questions.

I encourage students to revise with a red pencil so they can see how much they have added. We come back together the next day and talk about our experiences. Students agree that having a partner ask questions really helped them revise their stories for adding details. Students read and share their new stories so their classmates can see all the revisions.

Final Thoughts

Questions are great springboards for elaboration. When teachers ask themselves questions as they write, they model for students the importance of stopping, rereading, and considering the possibility of telling more. Engaging students in asking questions during shared writing experiences, as well as during individual writing conferences, encourages students to "try it out"—to use questions as tools to dig deeper and expand upon ideas.

USING ANECDOTES, EXAMPLES, DEFINITIONS, AND FACTS TO ELABORATE

It is several years back and I am sitting in a meeting with other teachers and administrators from around the state. Nikki Elliott-Schuman, writing expert from our Office for the Superintendent of Public Instruction (OSPI), is sharing the latest "aha's" from last spring's WASL (Washington Assessment of Student Learning) tests. There are many things to celebrate, and we do, but we are also here to listen to ways in which our students can improve. The wonderful thing about Nikki is she doesn't just share weaknesses. She presents ammunition for addressing those weaknesses. One of the areas she focuses on today is elaboration. Our students are not elaborating on their ideas as much as they could. Nikki shares a list of strategies for elaborating:

- Anecdote
- Example
- Definition
- Description
- Quotation
- Statistics
- Facts

I scan the list and some ideas are familiar. I teach my students to use description, and to "slow down the moment" by including what someone says or how someone feels (see Chapter 4). But some of the other ideas on the list are not ones I have taught to my primary students.

My eyes focus on anecdotes. "Hmm," I think. I never considered teaching my students to use anecdotes as a way to elaborate. After all, my students are just second graders. This is far above their ability level. Or is it?

Using Anecdotes to Elaborate

Back in my classroom, my first thought focuses on how to define *anecdote* for young writers. *Webster's Dictionary* defines *anecdote* as "a short account of an interesting or amusing incident or event, often biographical." I think of terms my students will understand. An anecdote is really a short personal story. I explain to them that when they use an anecdote to elaborate, they are writing a story within a story.

Then I share this example with them. "If I say, 'My grandmother was a funny woman,' I can elaborate by adding a list of details such as these: Her jokes were funny. She was a prankster and loved playing tricks on people. She said funny things and made the most outrageous faces."

"Or," I continue, "I could take a different approach and say, 'My grandmother was a funny woman' and elaborate by telling you about a specific time she did something funny." Here's the example I share with them.

Anecdotes as a Way of Elaborating

MODELS FROM

L I T E R A T U R E

CHAPTER BOOKS

"'This cousin of hers built a web across a stream. One day she was hanging around on the web and a tiny fish leaped into the air and got tangled in the web. The fish was caught by one fin, Mother; its tail was wildly thrashing . . . .'"

—*Charlotte's Web*, by E. B. White, p. 106

"They were kind, especially Julie. I remember that when one rat was being tagged, she looked at it and said, 'Poor little thing, he's frightened. Look how he's trembling.'"

—*Mrs. Frisby and the Rats of NIMH*, by Robert C. O'Brien, p. 110

"Life is far more interesting in the woods than on the front porch! One time Bobby tried to stow some garden snakes in his T-shirt, and they latched on to his stomach. Mom had to put her foot against him to get enough leverage to pull them off..."

—*The Green Dog*, by Suzanne Fisher Staples, p. 51

PICTURE BOOKS

• *Abe Lincoln's Hat*, by Martha Brenner, pp. 13–14, 16–17
• *A Picture Book of Helen Keller*, by David Adler, p. 10
• *Raewyn's Got the Writing Bug Again*, by Raewyn Caisley, p. 4
• *Thank You, Mr. Falker*, by Patricia Polacco, pp. 8, 9
• *Van Gogh*, by Mike Venezia, p. 20

My grandmother was a funny woman. One time we were at the dry cleaning counter, paying for her clean clothes. A woman in line was very fidgety, and as my grandmother was counting out her money, she muttered, "Hurry up."

Well, my grandmother turned around and said, "Listen, lady. Don't get your panties tied in a knot." We began to giggle and by the time we were out the door, we were laughing full-out.

By using an anecdote in the second version, I was definitely able to tell more about the kind of woman my grandmother was.

Other examples I share with students use different cue words to start the anecdotes, such as *sometimes* and *I remember*.

I like taking walks in lovely places. Sometimes I go through the woods by my house where beautiful trees and flowers grow. I smell the flowers and look up at the tall trees, standing like giants. I watch for sudden surprises, like a butterfly landing on a leaf, or a worm wiggling in the dirt.

My dad is a huge Red Sox fan. I remember a time when we went to a Red Sox game. My dad cheered for every player as they went up to bat. He wore his Red Sox shirt and hat. He told everyone around us all the old Red Sox stories.

CONNECTING TO TEXT I start with what I know works best—sharing examples of elaboration using anecdotes that come from real literature. Because of the nature of anecdotes, it makes sense to look first in biographies, autobiographies, and memoirs. I search the books in my classroom for anecdotes. Right away I find a few and, lo and behold, many use the words "One time" to start the anecdotes.

In *A Picture Book of Harriet Tubman*, David Adler describes how Harriet despised slavery. He tells us that she didn't like doing as she was told. Then, using the words *one time*, Adler tells an anecdote about a time Harriet stole a lump of sugar from a bowl when she was hired out to work. The passage goes on to share how Harriet never had tasted anything that sweet. Adler continues telling how Harriet was chased with a whip by her mistress for that act.

I read this passage to students and ask them to listen as writers, as well as readers.

"What does the author, David Adler, tell us about Harriet Tubman?" I ask.

Malcolm answers, "That she didn't like to do as she was told."

I agree and ask, "Does he stop there or does he tell us more?"

Students agree, "He tells more."

"How does Adler do this?" I continue.

Emma says, "He tells us she didn't do what she was told—when she took the sugar from the bowl—and got whipped."

Jessica adds, "He says, 'One time . . .' and then tells us about the time she disobeyed."

"Right," I say. "It's kind of like a little story within the story about Harriet Tubman. Why do you think the author does this?"

Johnny says, "To make it more interesting."

"So we know her better," adds Ryan.

"This could be. David Adler is telling a story within a story in his book about Harriet Tubman. He uses the words *one time* to begin his 'story within a story.' Other words that work are *once, sometimes,* and *I remember when.*"

I continue sharing anecdotes from other books. I hope these will serve as inspiration for students as they try to include anecdotes as a way of elaborating in their writing.

> CUES WRITERS USE WHEN ELABORATING WITH ANECDOTES
>
> ✓ One time . . .
>
> ✓ Sometimes . . .
>
> ✓ Once . . .
>
> ✓ I remember when . . .

MINI-LESSON

CONNECTING TO A PAST LESSON

Mini-lessons that connect to past lessons can be very powerful. Here is one that was successful with my students.

Introduce the Purpose for the Lesson/ Connecting to Past Lesson

While I rarely assign a topic for writing, I want students to have an opportunity to try using an anecdote. Some topics and genres lend themselves to including anecdotes, so I suggest that we write about our favorite places. And so we talk about those, after reading *All the Places to Love*, by Patricia MacLachlan. Students share "Disneyland", "my backyard", "our cabin", "my bed", "the baseball field," among others. I write "Our Favorite Places" on a class chart and record student ideas (see Figure 6.1).

The next day I tell students I am going to write about one of my favorite places. I turn to our chart for ideas and think aloud my process for deciding on a place.

"Well, I love Disneyland, but that's a pretty big place and it might be difficult to stay focused. I love to dance so I could write about being on a dance floor. That's not on our chart. I just thought of it. Yesterday, I shared that I love my couch. It's warm and comfortable. It's not a big place but sometimes small places are good topics. I think I will write about my couch."

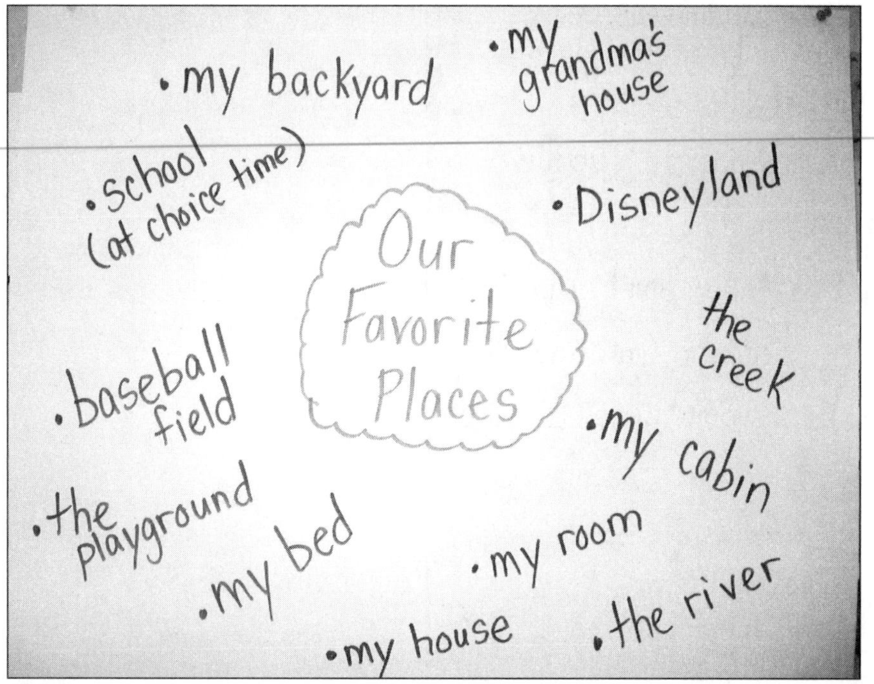

Figure 6.1
Student-generated list of favorite places.

I tell my story first, including that I love to read on my couch, I take naps on it, and I love to curl up with a blanket and watch TV from my couch. My couch is white and soft.

Modeling

I begin by modeling a clear first sentence: *One of my favorite places is my soft, white couch.* Then I think aloud as I elaborate, adding details about what my couch looks and feels like, and what I do there. When I get to: *I like to take naps,* I add, "One time I slept for three hours. I slept right through dinner. I must have been really tired!"

I am modeling for students a simple one- or two-line anecdote. That's where we start. I want this to be attainable, so I begin small. As students help me reread my piece to see if it makes sense, we realize I used an anecdote (a *One time . . .*). We also realize I need to add an ending sentence, so I do: *I just love my couch.* Once that's done I encourage students to use a "One time . . ." anecdote to elaborate in their writing. As they tell about their favorite places, I prod them to think about a particular time they were there, and tell that "story within their story."

As figures 6.2 and 6.3 on the next page show, student writing is a wonderful model for mini-lessons. If a student succeeds in elaborating by using an anecdote (or anything else), I have him or her co-teach a subsequent mini-lesson with me. There is nothing like a classmate's well-done work to inspire young writers.

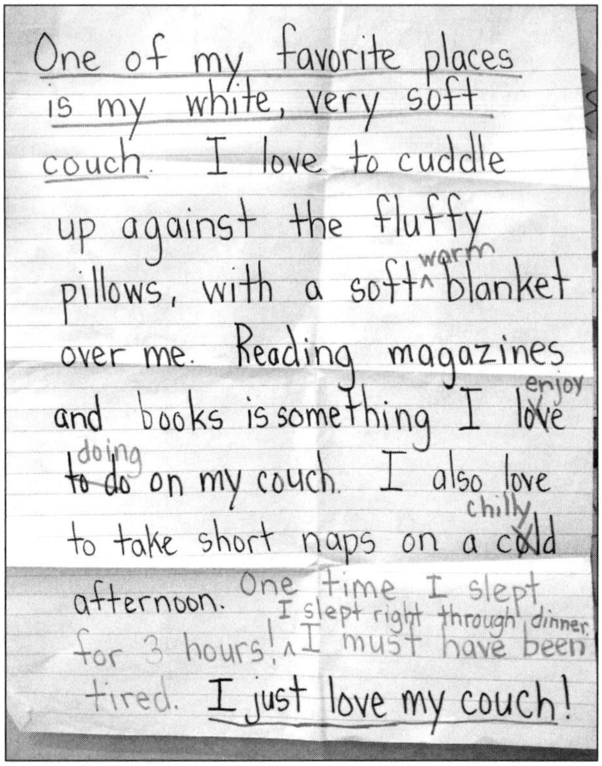

One of my favorite places is my white, very soft couch. I love to cuddle up against the fluffy pillows, with a soft warm blanket over me. Reading magazines and books is something I love enjoy to do doing on my couch. I also love to take short naps on a cold chilly afternoon. One time I slept for 3 hours! I slept right through dinner. I must have been tired. I just love my couch!

Figure 6.2
Writing about my favorite place

My favorite place to go is the rocks on orcas island beach where the crabs nest, seastars are. If you look at the sea stars close they look like a rainbow. Some times I take off my socks and shos I pat my feet in the ocean. I.V seen pink, purple, oran and yellow seastars there squshy. Onee I was standing on a lose rock and fell with my cloths on! I stay away from crabs there beacase I don't want to get pinched!!! I love Orcas Island beach!

Figure 6.3
Emelia includes an anecdote in her writing about Orcas Island.

Using Examples to Elaborate

"Examples are an effective way to help the reader understand what you are talking about." (Washington State Office for the Superintendent of Public Instruction)

The use of examples is another technique for elaborating on ideas. Examples are often found in nonfiction texts, but can also be found in fiction. Examples are just that— examples. If I want to say, "My garden is full of lovely flowers," I can elaborate by adding examples, so the sentence reads:

My garden is full of lovely flowers: tulips, daffodils, roses, and gardenias.

I simply add a colon and then list specific examples. Here's another:

We had all sorts of weather in that one hour: rain, hail, snow, and sun.

Sometimes writers actually use the words, "for example."

Husky football fans are full of school spirit. For example, every time there's a touchdown, they sing the school song, "Bow Down to Washington."

Or:

My dog is very protective. For example, he stands in front of me and barks when a stranger comes near.

Another cue that writers use when they want to include an example is "for instance."

Baseball is a very difficult sport. For instance, players have to be able to hit a ball that is coming toward them at 90 mph.

CONNECTING TO TEXT Again, I look in books to find how authors use examples as a way to elaborate. I read several to the class, and we discuss the cue words the author chose to use, and how this technique adds to a piece of writing.

After stating that many stories about bats are not true, Seymour Simon, in *Amazing Bats*, uses the words *for example* to elaborate, revealing that bats are not blind.

I ask students, "What does the author tell us about bats?"

Robbie answers, "That lots of stories about bats aren't true."

"Yes. How does he elaborate on this statement?"

Bobby answers, "He tells you one thing that isn't true: bats are not blind."

I continue, "So he gives you an example of a story about bats that isn't true. In fact, I notice, he actually uses the words, *for example,* before he tells you bats aren't blind."

Students notice this too.

MODELS FROM

L I T E R A T U R E

CHAPTER BOOKS

"Once Egyptians found a way to do something, they stuck with it. They didn't try to improve things or make progress for its own sake. For example, it might take 100 men to move around a heavy stone building block. Since 100 workers were always available to do this . . ."

—*Egypt,* by Stephen Krensky, pp. 25–26

"Though he killed bats—even ate their eggs—what Marty liked to hunt were other four-legged creatures, like mice, rats, rabbits, and squirrels."

—*Ereth's Birthday,* by Avi, pp. 11–12.

"For the first time they used sounds along with the shapes, and pictures, real pictures we could recognize. For example, one of the first and simplest of these exercises was a picture, a clear photograph, of a rat."

—*Mrs. Frisby and the Rats of NIMH,* by Robert C. O'Brien, p. 122

"Every action, reader, no matter how small, has a consequence. For instance, the young Roscuro gnawed on Gregory the jailer's rope, and because he gnawed on the rope, a match was lit in his face, and because a match was lit in his face, his soul was set afire."

—*The Tale of Despereaux,* by Kate DiCamillo, p. 117

". . . and it [the barn] was full of all sorts of things that you find in barns: ladders, grindstones, pitch forks, monkey wrenches, scythes, lawn mowers, snow shovels, ax handles, milk pails, water buckets, empty grain sacks, and rusty rat traps."

—*Charlotte's Web,* by E. B. White, pp. 13–14

"Mingled with the sharp scent of pine and fir, she breathed in delicious hints of good things to eat: nuts, berries, seeds, fragrant flowers, tender roots."

—*Poppy,* by Avi, p. 107

PICTURE BOOKS

• *A Freshwater Pond,* by Adam Hibbert, p. 21
• *Spinning Spiders,* by Melvin Berger, p. 20
• *A Whale Is Not a Fish and Other Animal Mix-ups,* by Melvin Berger, p. 12
• *Weather,* by Seymour Simon, p. 14

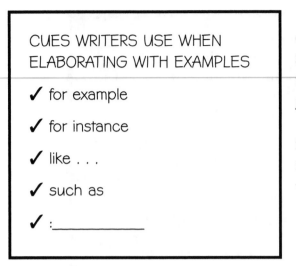

"Sometimes," I tell students, "authors will elaborate on an idea by giving examples. Sometimes, they actually use specific words to tell you the example is coming, like: *for example, for instance,* or *such as.*"

I encourage students to look for books that include examples as a way of elaborating. Students search out books and find multiple ways authors use examples in their writing.

◆

MINI-LESSON

LINKING WRITING TO SOCIAL STUDIES

Writing mini-lessons can be born out of content area study. The following mini-lesson stems from a social studies unit on people of courage.

Introduce the Purpose for the Lesson

Many of my mini-lessons are born out of student interest and student suggestion. We were studying the genre of biography in reading workshop. Students were reading about some extraordinary people, such as Harriet Tubman, Chief Joseph, Martin Luther King, Jr., and Helen Keller. I read, we read together, and students participated in literature circles, studying about real people in history. This reading workshop unit led to a shared writing lesson using examples to elaborate. We decided to write a book about Harriet Tubman for students in other classrooms. One of our goals was to see whether we could elaborate upon at least one idea, using an example.

Shared Writing

Of course, we began at the beginning. I suggested we start with a clear first sentence so our reader would know what our book was about. I asked, "Any ideas?"

Tatum said, "We should say something that shows Harriet was an interesting person."

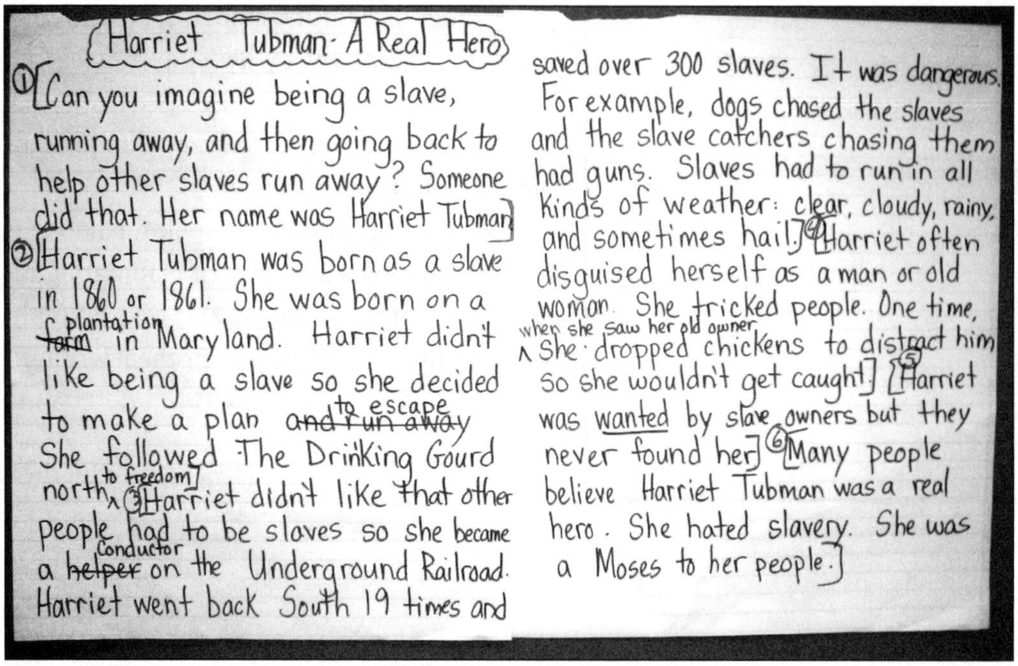

Figure 6.4
Writing about Harriet Tubman in shared writing.

Josh suggested, "Why don't we start with a question?"

"Good idea," I said. "Do you have one in mind?"

Josh continued, "How about, 'Can you imagine being a slave, running away, and then going back to help other slaves run away?'"

"I love it," I answered. To include Tatum, I asked her, "What could we add to let readers know who we are writing about?"

Tatum said, "We can say, 'Someone did that. Her name was Harriet Tubman. This is her story.'" I record the sentences on our chart, and we have a lead.

I remind students that this is a biography and ask, "How are biographies organized? How do they start?" Students agree that authors usually tell when and where the person was born. We decide to begin there too. 'Harriet Tubman was born as a slave

Figure 6.5
Picture of student-written book about Harriet Tubman.

in 1860 or 1861. She was born in Maryland.'

We work our way through our ideas, thinking about all we learned about this famous person. We decide on a clear sequence, and continue writing, working to elaborate upon each idea. When we get to the part about Harriet helping slaves escape, Sean wants to add, "It was danger-ous." Here, I find my opportunity to guide students to use an example to elaborate.

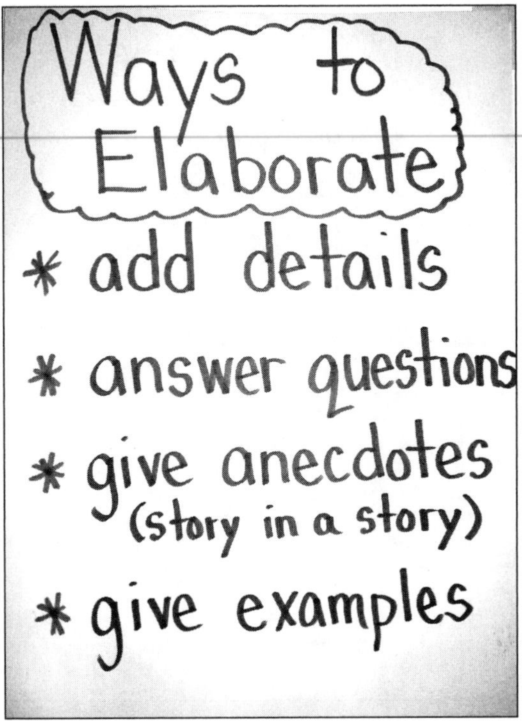

I say, "That's a great idea." Then I suggest, "This might be a great place to add, *for example*."

Students agree and Nick says, "For example, dogs chased them."

Adena adds, "And the slave catchers had guns."

Ways to Elaborate

* add details

* answer questions

* give anecdotes (story in a story)

* give examples

Figure 6.6 *Our Ways to Elaborate chart.*

As we work to record Nick's and Adena's ideas, students help to make the sentences read smoothly:

> It was dangerous. For example, dogs chased the slaves, and the slave catchers chasing them had guns.

Students also remember an example I shared about different kinds of weather, using a colon before the examples. They modify it for our story here.

> Slaves had to run in all kinds of weather: clear, cloudy, rainy, and sometimes windy.

We finish our piece, revising, editing, and finally publishing it as a book for neighboring classrooms (see figures 6.4 and 6.5). And we add *examples* to our growing list of Ways to Elaborate.

Here's how Linnae used examples when she wrote about pumpkins.

> **Did you know there are lots of different kinds of pumpkins like Small Sugar Pie, Red October, Trick-or-Treat, Jack Be Little, Baby Bear, and Big Max?**
>
> **—Linnae, second grade**

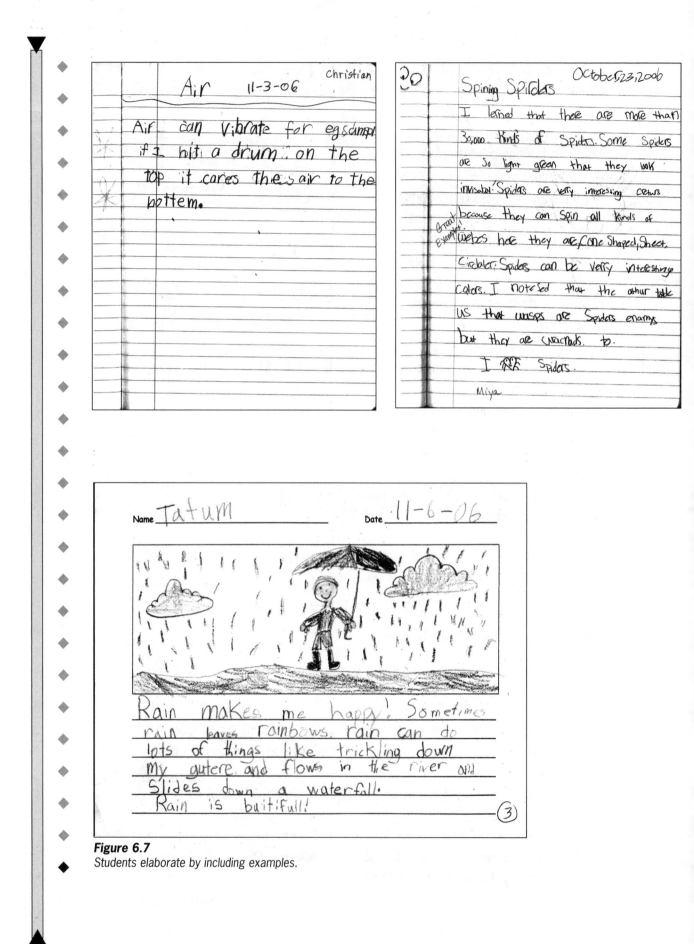

Figure 6.7

Students elaborate by including examples.

Using Definitions to Elaborate

Authors often elaborate by including definitions, or explanations about a word, topic, or concept. When authors do this, they are showing a real awareness of audience. These definitions clarify for the reader, but they also elaborate upon the idea presented.

For example,

Owls are predators. That means they hunt other animals, eating them to survive.

or

Owls are predators, which means they hunt other animals, eating them to survive.

or

Owls are predators. Predators hunt other animals, eating them to survive.

CUES WRITERS USE WHEN
ELABORATING WITH DEFINITIONS

✓ that means

✓ this is

✓ which means

✓ _____ are

✓ like

When we encourage students to look for definitions in the books they read, they find that authors often elaborate using this technique. Over several days, during reading workshop, I ask students to record any definitions they find in the books they read. We share these as examples of how authors elaborate.

CONNECTING TO TEXT I revisit a book I used with one of my guided reading groups. The book is *Frogs and Toads and Tadpoles, Too*, by Allan Fowler. In the small group, one of my students, Robbie, notices a new word: *amphibian*. He asks, "What's an amphibian?"

I suggest, "Keep reading. You might find out by clues in the text."

Robbie becomes very excited when the next sentence tells him what he wants to know. "Oh," he says. "It just told us."

"You're right. After telling us that frogs and toads are amphibians, the author actually tells us what an amphibian is by using the words 'that means', and then giving us the definition of an amphibian." I decide to read the book to the whole class.

After finishing our guided reading group, I ask Robbie if he will help me teach an elaboration lesson to the rest of the class. He agrees.

Using Definitions as a Way to Elaborate

CHAPTER BOOKS

"The king stopped singing. He squinted. The king was nearsighted; that is, anything that was not right in front of his eyes was very difficult for him to see."

— *The Tale of Despereaux*, by Kate DiCamillo, p. 28

"Wolves are predators. Predators are hunters and must eat meat to survive."

— *Wolves*, by Carolyn B. Otto, p. 39

"All reptiles are cold-blooded. That means their blood stays the same temperature as the air around them."

— *Snakes!*, by the Editors of TIME FOR KIDS with Lisa Jo Rudy, p. 6

"Just off the shore from the coastline stand tall seastacks. They are columns of rock that were once part of the mainland."

— *Olympic National Park*, by Sharlene and Ted Nelson, p. 14

"The sun has gravity. Gravity is a force that attracts all objects to one another. The sun's gravity pulls on the planets and moons.

—*Solar System*, by Gregory Vogt, p. 7

PICTURE BOOKS

• *Are You a Grasshopper?*, by Judy Allen and Tudor Humphries, p. 31
• *Barefoot (Author's Note)*, by Pamela Duncan Edwards, p. 30
• *Wolves*, by Gail Gibbons, pp. 8, 11

We review how authors elaborate. Students mention:

a story in a story

details

examples

Then I tell the class, "Some of our students found another way authors elaborate." I ask Robbie to read the sentences from our book to see if classmates can figure it out.

Robbie reads, "'Frogs and toads are amphibians. That means they live on both land and water.'"

I ask, "What is the first thing the author says?"

Adena answers, "He tells us frogs and toads are amphibians."

"Yes, and then what does he do?"

"He tells us what amphibians are—that they live on land and in water," adds Josh.

"Yes. He actually gives the reader the definition of an amphibian, in case you don't know what one is. That is the way he elaborates or adds a detail. He gives a definition and he does this by using the words 'that means' beforehand."

Again, I encourage students to go on an elaboration hunt—this time looking for definitions. "Where can you find places authors use definitions as a way of elaborating?"

STUDENT EXAMPLES

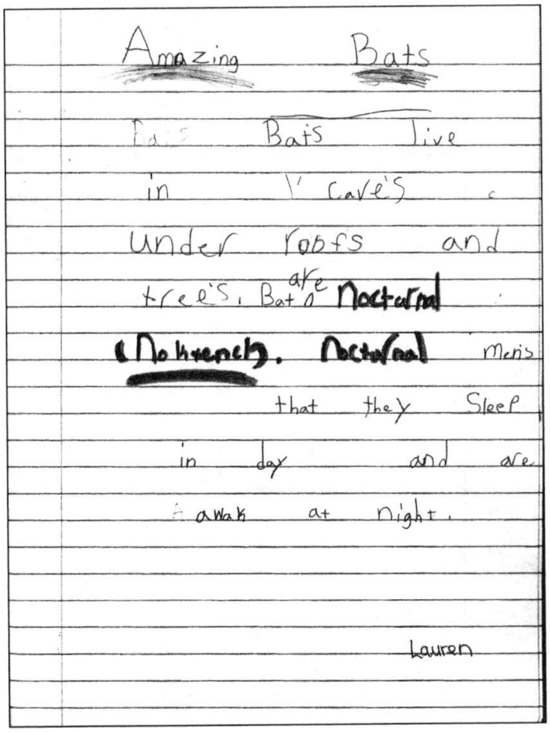

Figure 6.8
Students include definitions to elaborate.

We road hunted. I went with my dad and grandpa. He is 81 and my dad is 51. We drove the thunderbird. It is red. I brought my pellet gun and bebe gun too. We had to get up at 2 in the morning. It was dark still. It was a 6 hour drive to Eastern Washington. We went hunting for deer. We caught a deer. <u>Road hunting is when you sit in your car and put your gun in your lap and look for deer in your car.</u> The first day we stayed at a hotel.

—from "My Hunting Trip "
by Robbie, second grade

Figure 6.9
From second grader Jordan's book titled "Do You Like Cats?"

Using Facts and Statistics to Elaborate

Facts and statistics can be very powerful strategies for elaborating. They can accentuate a point, strengthen a statement, or just entertain us with a "wow" factor. If I tell you that Bill Gates is the richest man in the world, I can add that he has a net worth of $59 billion. That added statistic piques the reader's interest. Likewise, if I say the Red Sox experienced a long dry spell before winning the World Series, I can elaborate by telling you that before 2004, the Red Sox last won the World Series in 1918. That fact supports my original statement and is an effective way of elaborating on an idea.

We want to teach students to elaborate by using facts or statistics, when doing so will build upon their ideas. When students write for state assessments, they are encouraged to use facts and statistics; they are even allowed to make them up.

> FACTS AND STATISTICS
>
> ✓ often include numbers
>
> ✓ consist of factual statements (not opinions)

CONNECTING TO TEXT I encourage students to look for facts and statistics mentioned in the books they read. I start with animal nonfiction because these books are high interest for most students, and they often include the addition of facts as a way of elaborating. I tell students to look for numbers, as well as factual statements.

When students are ready, I begin with a book such as *The Journey of a Turtle,* by Carolyn Scrace. On page 12, Scrace states that turtles start to migrate when the weather gets colder. She writes that they are very strong swimmers, adding that they swim over 1500 miles during their journey.

I ask students, "What does this paragraph tell us?"

Johnny says, "Turtles migrate when it gets cold."

"Right," I answer. "Anything else?"

Emelia says, "They're strong swimmers. And some of them swim over 1500 miles when they migrate."

I respond, "Yes. This author tells us turtles are strong swimmers. Then she elaborates by giving a fact (or statistic), telling us some turtles swim 1500 miles on their migration journey."

I continue, "Often, especially in nonfiction books like this, authors add details about how high an animal can jump, how many bugs it

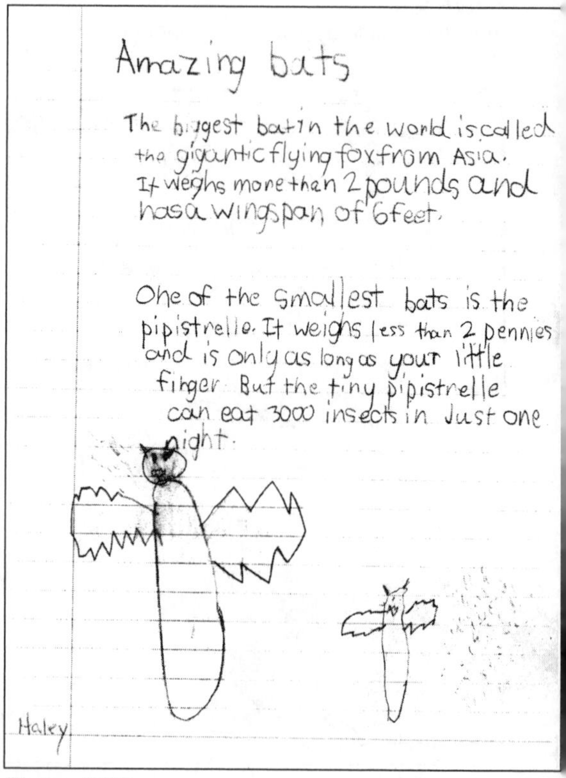
Amazing bats

The biggest bat in the world is called the gigantic flying fox from Asia. It weighs more than 2 pounds and has a wingspan of 6 feet.

One of the smallest bats is the pipistrelle. It weighs less than 2 pennies and is only as long as your little finger. But the tiny pipistrelle can eat 3000 insects in just one night.

Haley

Figure 6.10
Haley used statistics to elaborate when she wrote about flying foxes.

MODELS FROM

L I T E R A T U R E

CHAPTER BOOKS

"We live on the third planet from the sun. Our home is mostly covered with water. The land is made of rock and soil."

—*Solar System,* by Gregory Vogt, p. 14

"Gemstones can be very valuable. One diamond called the Millennium Star is worth at least $100 million! This big diamond is 2 inches (5 cm) long."

—*Rocks and Minerals,* by Kris Hirschmann, p. 8

"A prairie dog is about twice as big as a gray tree squirrel. An adult prairie dog weighs between two and four pounds. And from the tip of its nose to the tip of its tail, a prairie dog measures between 15 and 19 inches."

—*Prairie Dogs,* by Caroline Arnold, p. 4

"Venomous snakes poison their prey. They use their fangs to inject venom when they bite. Spitting cobras also spray their venom. They can spit venom from their fangs at an enemy eight feet away!"

—*Snakes!,* by the Editors of TIME FOR KIDS, p. 22

PICTURE BOOKS

• *Amazing Bats,* by Seymour Simon, pp. 5, 8, 19

• *Life in the Polar Lands,* by Monica Byles, pp. 9, 12, 15

• *Haiku Hike,* by fourth graders at St. Mary's Catholic School, Mansfield, MA, pp. 11, 17, 23

• *Wonders of the Desert,* by Louis Sabin, pp. 11, 19

eats in a day, or how fast or far it can swim. These details are called statistics. This is another way authors elaborate."

Again, we are off on a search. How many facts and statistics can we find? It is amazing to see the number of times authors choose to elaborate by using facts and statistics.

Figure 6.10 shows a great example of how students can use statistics to elaborate and enrich their writing.

Final Thoughts

Asking students to elaborate on an idea is a very vague proposition. When we break apart some ways writers choose to elaborate—sharing an anecdote, example, definition, or statistic—and then teach these as strategies for students to use in their own writing, we give students real options. We teach students that there are specific ways they can learn to elaborate upon their ideas.

CONFERENCES AND ELABORATION: SIDE-BY-SIDE MINI-LESSONS

Each year students come to us with varying levels of writing experience and ability. Some first graders have written in kindergarten; some have not. Some come with knowledge of sounds and letters, maybe already reading, and some are still working on recognizing the alphabet. Some second, third, and fourth graders dislike writing when they enter our classrooms and some have kept a journal all summer, filled with stories and poems and letters. There are students who write when they have to and those who write every chance they get. And some students are working on learning to write in English because it is their second language.

Like you, I strive to meet the needs of all my students, as varied as they are. While I try to teach lessons that will touch each of them, I can't possibly give every student all that I need to, without having some really personal one-on-one time. This personal time is the writing conference.

Lucy Calkins says, "If a teacher can listen to a writer talk about her writing . . . and intervene in ways that lift the level not only of the piece of writing but of the child's work on future pieces, that teacher's conferences are a Very Big Deal" (2005).

I strive to make my conferences a "Very Big Deal." I observe students and their writing, and figure out what comes next. In

Conferring with one of my students.

this chapter I will share some one-on-one conferences. I have chosen conferences that focus on choosing topics and adding details. Of course, there are many other things I address in writing conferences, but my focus here will be on these two aspects of writing.

I sit very close to students during writing conferences. I lean in. Yet the student is ultimately in charge. I ask her, "What do you want to talk about?" Her paper, book, or journal remains in her hand. She reads to me. It is a conversation that leads us, rather than a question, answer, question, answer.

Conference One: Choosing a Topic

Tony cannot think of a topic, again. This seems to be a common theme for him. He sits with his journal turned to a blank page. I let him sit awhile, giving him a chance to mull over things. As teachers, we want to go in and save the day right away. For those without topics, we want to give them something to write about, or come with a handful of suggestions. I'm not saying that making suggestions isn't a good thing, but sometimes we are too quick to rescue students. We don't give them a chance to think on their own and rescue themselves. If we are always there right away to help with a topic, those students will always depend on us for that and never become independent.

As I watch Tony sit a bit longer, I realize he is ready for a conference. "What's up, Tony?" I ask as I sit down next to him. Tony shrugs his shoulders.

"What are you writing about today?" I ask.

"I don't know," he answers. "I can't think of anything."

"Hmm. That seems to be a problem. What have we learned about what makes a good topic? Do you remember?"

Tony looks at our chart titled "What Makes a Good Topic," which hangs in the room. He answers, "Something you know or something you like."

"Right. Does anything pop into your head right now?"

"No," Tony says quickly.

"Okay, let's just talk then. Sometimes talking can help you think of an idea. What have you been doing lately at home?"

"Not much," he says.

"Hey, I saw your mom up at school last night walking a dog. Whose dog is that?"

"Oh, that's Lady. That's our dog now."

"Tell me about her. When did you get her?"

"We went to the shelter last weekend and got her. She had nobody else."

"So how did that happen?" I ask.

Tony explains, "My mom's friend went to the shelter and got a dog, and then she told my mom about this other dog that was there that needed a home."

I begin to ask questions, but they come as part of a conversation with Tony. "So tell me about her. What kind of dog is she? She's not a puppy. How old is she? Do you know why she was left at the shelter?" Tony answers the questions and we talk about his new dog.

"You know, Tony, I think Lady would make a great writing topic. She is someone you know about and someone you like. You told me lots about her. I would love if you wrote down some of your ideas". Tony agrees and begins writing.

Students don't always recognize the things in their lives that make good topics. It is important that we have conversations with them, so they may discover topics for themselves. Sometimes it takes a simple nudge: "I notice you were not happy about the popcorn sales changing days. How could that turn into a piece of writing for you?" Or, "I notice you are becoming quite the expert on wolves. You've been reading a lot of books about wolves. I bet you could write your own great nonfiction book using all you have learned." Or simply, "I notice you lost a tooth. That would make a great topic." Students appreciate that we are observant of their likes and dislikes, and they don't mind when we make a suggestion now and again.

Conference Two: Adding Text to a Picture

Early writers are usually able to draw a picture with varying degrees of detail. For those who draw simple pictures with no text, I encourage adding details to their pictures. We talk about their drawings, and usually they say something I don't see on the paper. I suggest they add the detail to their story by drawing it in the picture. Detail also comes in the form of color, so I might suggest a different-color marker or crayon to add more detail.

For those students who are ready to write something, whether letters match sounds or not, I nudge them to think of words or a sentence that tells the story of their picture.

Katie is in kindergarten. She is an average student who is not very confident when it comes to writing. Katie has her first wiggly tooth. She knows that good topics are ones you know and like. She knows about a wiggly tooth, and because it is her first wiggly tooth, she is excited about this; it makes the perfect topic. She draws a picture.

I sit down with Katie and say, "Tell me about your picture."

Katie says, "My tooth is wiggly."

"I know. How exciting for you! Oh. I see three pictures here. Tell me about each one."

Katie points to the middle picture. "This is me and here is where I lost my tooth." She points to the picture on the left. "Here is my face and you can see where my tooth is wiggly." Then, pointing to the picture on the right, "Here is my tooth."

"Wow, you have a lot of details in your pictures. If you were to write a sentence to go with your picture, what would you say?" I ask.

Katie thinks and says, "My tooth is wiggly."

"That's a great sentence. Would you like to write it so that your readers will know your message?"

Figure 7.1
Katie's picture and writing.

Katie begins sounding out the words. She looks to me for approval for each letter she writes. After she has written her sentence, I ask her to read it back to me.

All of a sudden, Katie starts adding another sentence. She says "I'm five." (See Figure 7.1.)

She writes what she hears and then says, "Wait." She makes a mark after the "m" in "I'm." She is writing an apostrophe. She doesn't write it in the correct place, but the fact that she knows a special mark belongs somewhere impresses me.

Katie rereads her new piece to me. I praise her for adding text to her picture. "Katie, I am so happy you decided to write a sentence with your picture. And you added a detail too! You have so many details in your pictures, as well. Good writers think of sentences to write that match the ideas in their pictures. Then they work on adding details, just like you did."

Conference Three: Adding a Detail

As students become comfortable with letters and sounds, and the notion that writers write a sentence to go with their picture, I nudge them to add a detail or two to their writing.

J. T. is an energetic first grader with a love for animals. J. T. loves to draw and until recently did not want to add text to his pictures. His pictures are filled with lots of details including many colors. Today J. T chooses to draw and write about dinosaurs. When my teaching partner, Cynthia Heffernan, sits down to confer with him, he is finished with his picture and has written, "Dinosaurs lived for 1000 years ago and died one trillion years ago."

Cynthia says, "Tell me about your picture, J. T." These words are priceless. They are unassuming. They immediately put the child in charge of the conference.

J. T. begins describing his picture. "Here is the big dinosaur. He eats leaves. And here is the littler dinosaur. He has spikes because he is mean, and he uses them to attack."

Cynthia continues, "What is this over here?"

J. T. answers, "This is another dinosaur that is big, and he might want to fight the other big dinosaur for the leaves."

"Oh my, you really have a lot of details in your picture. All of your colors really add to your picture. How did you decide which colors to choose?"

"I just chose them," says J. T

Cynthia now focuses on the text. "Would you read what you wrote?"

J. T reads, "Dinosaurs lived for one thousand years ago and died one trillion years ago." Even though this sentence does not make a lot of sense, Cynthia knows J.T. made an attempt to add writing to his picture, on his own. She chooses not to explore the reliability of the statement and says instead, "That is very interesting. They did live and die a long time ago. You know, J. T., you said a lot of other things about your picture. Authors often write a very interesting fact about their picture and then add a detail. Would you like to add a detail in writing?"

Figure 7.2
J. T. revises his writing by adding a detail.

"Sure," J. T agrees.

"What would you like to add? Let's reread your sentence." J. T does this. "What else could you say?"

J. T answers, "Some were big and some were small."

Cynthia says, "That's a great detail and it goes along with your picture beautifully."

J. T writes his detail, sounding out the words (see Figure 7.2). Cynthia praises him and says, "You just revised by adding a detail. Revising is when an author changes their original writing to make it better. You did that when you added another sentence."

Conference Four: Gathering Ideas

Sometimes students can write, but they don't know how to settle on an idea with enough details to write something of length. Often this student can't pick a topic because he does not know if he will have enough to say about the topic. This student not only needs help in choosing a topic, but in gathering ideas and planning for his writing.

Ricky looks around the room. His paper is blank. He fidgets a bit with his pencil, twisting it back and forth. His eyes rest on Ashley's drawing. He notices she is beginning to write about her picture. Across from Ricky, Sean and Robbie seem to have started their own projects; Sean is writing an animal book, and Robbie is writing about his camping trip.

Ricky licks his lips and sighs. I observe this from across the room. I see the frustration on Ricky's face, frustration over not being able to think of a topic. I drop in, readying myself for a conversation.

"What do we have here, Ricky?"

"Nothing. I can't think of anything to write."

"Really?" I ask. "Tell me something you did last weekend."

Ricky thinks a minute and says, "We played baseball."

"Wow! I love baseball. I used to play on a team. Do you have a team?" Ricky nods.

"What is the name of your team?"

"The Indians," Ricky says.

"Oh. May I write this down so we remember?" I write down "Indians."

"What position do you play?"

"I play everywhere, but my favorite is first and second base."

"Write that down here." I point to the paper. As Ricky writes I tell him I used to play second base.

I continue asking questions. "What else can you tell me?"

Ricky answers, "We play with a pitching machine."

"You do! Tell me about it."

Ricky continues, "It's kind of hard and kind of not. I hit a home run once."

"You did! Wow! Both of those are interesting details. How did you feel when you hit your home run?" I ask.

"I felt good. It was when we played against Alex's team," Ricky answers.

I urge Ricky to write a word or two for each of his ideas. I tell him these words will help remind him of the things he wants to write. I point out that while he just wrote "pitching machine" on his paper, when he sees that, it will help him think of the detail —about it being "kind of hard and kind of not hard." When he sees "home run," he might think of playing Alex's team and how it felt good to hit the home run. I tell Ricky, "These words are just the main ideas. When you write them into sentences, think of how you can elaborate. Tell how you feel, what you see, why it is hard or easy, why you like these positions best. I take him over to our Ways to Elaborate poster. We go down the list:

- tell why

- tell how

- tell what you see

- tell where

- tell who

I ask Ricky, "Do you know how you might like to start your piece? What would make a good first sentence?"

"I like to play baseball?" Ricky says.

I reassure him, "That sounds like a great first sentence. It will tell your reader what your story is going to be about." (See Figure 7.3.)

As I move to another student, Ricky begins writing.

Ricky had writer's block. We all get it, even the great authors. He was stuck and needed a nudge to figure out a topic, and to figure out some details to go with it. How can we teach that kind of personal lesson without homing in one on one? Yes, we can teach lessons that will generate possible writing topics. And we can teach lessons that will model how to think about what makes a good topic. But sometimes students need personal attention to help them figure out a topic. That is what Ricky needed: someone to listen to his ideas, help him figure out a topic, and gather details to make a story.

Conferences are key to the writing workshop. Some of the best mini-lessons occur here. You might be thinking, "Yes, Megan, but it's not very time-efficient to teach your lessons to one student at a time." I agree. That's why I teach most lessons to the whole or small group. However, this one-on-one time gives the teacher a chance to reach out directly to one child and celebrate, brainstorm, guide, question, and listen on a very personal level, one that is extremely meaningful for the student. I can't replace that experience with a whole-group lesson.

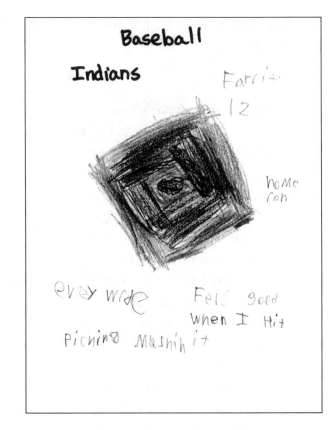

Figure 7.3
Ricky's planning sheet and finished writing.

Conference Five: Adding Details With Support

As students progress in writing, they want to add details. However, holding a conference in which we discuss a lot of ideas a student could add, and then saying, "Go back to your writing and add all of that," won't work. These students need our support. They need us to take notes about what they want to add; in essence, we become their secretaries.

Chase was not a confident writer when he came into first grade. He was very worried about writing the right letters. Chase did not write in kindergarten. He was reluctant with ideas because he didn't know how to write these ideas on paper. As the year progressed, Chase became more confident.

Today Chase has chosen a large 12- by 18-inch sheet of white construction paper to make his prewrite notes. He draws boxes on the paper. In each box, Chase writes a fact about an animal. He works for two days before he finally signs up for a conference.

"What do you have here, Chase?" I ask.

"It's about animals," he answers.

"I see that. I read from the top, 'Animals and Pets.' So this is a piece about animals and pets?"

Chase nods. "Yes."

I ask Chase to read his boxes to me. "Wow," I respond. You know a lot about these animals. You must have done some research." He nods. Then I say, "You know, Chase, these are great ideas but I have some questions that might help you add some details. Could you read each box to me again and I'll stop you when I have a question?" He agrees.

Chase reads from his first box. "Dogs. Dogs are playful and fun, but hard to take care of."

"Okay. Stop. Why are they hard to take care of?" I ask.

Chase answers, "Because you have to take them out to go to the bathroom."

I smile, amused. "Well that makes sense. I don't like getting up early to take my dog out to use the bathroom." I take out a sticky note. "Could I write that detail down and stick it right here next to your box?"

"Sure," he says.

"Okay. Read me the next box."

He begins, "Cats are playful but easier to take care of than dogs."

"All right. Why?"

He answers, "They have a litter box."

"Of course. Could I write that on a sticky note?" I place it next to the cat box. "Next box?"

Chase reads, "Frogs are slimy and eat bugs!"

"I agree. They are slimy. I have a question for you. How? How do they eat bugs?"

"They stick out their tongue and catch them," he answers.

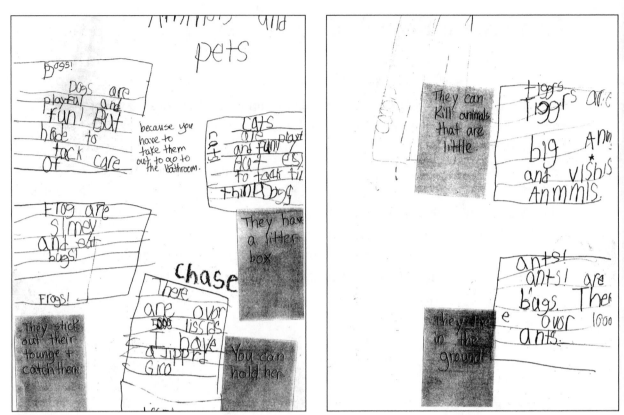

Figure 7.4
Chase's prewrite with sticky notes from a one-on-one conference.

I write on the sticky note and place it next to the frog box (see Figure 7.4). We continue with the boxes about lizards, tigers, and ants. Afterward, I suggest to Chase that he had so many more details to tell. By asking him questions like *how, why, what*, and *where* Chase was able to elaborate on his ideas. I chose to be his recorder because that was where Chase was in his ability to revise. He needed some support. These were his ideas. I just was his secretary.

I ask Chase to go back and reread his ideas, as they are written now. I tell him to see if there is anything else he would like to add. When Chase returns, he asks if we can publish this piece. "Of course," I say. You have done a lot of work on it. How would you like to publish it?"

Dogs are playful and fun! But hard to take care of because you have to let them out to go to the bathroom.	Cats are playful and fun! But easier to take care of than dogs. They have a litter box.

Figure 7.5
Two pages from Chase's typed book.

He answers, "In a book, each animal on a different page."

"Okay." When we set a time for Chase's publishing conference, he is right there with me as I type. He makes the decisions about where the text goes on the page. This side-by-side experience gives him another chance to make revisions, as he sees his work typed out on the page. (See Figure 7.5.)

Conference Six: Filling in Details

Here is another conference in which the student needs support from the teacher in recording her revisions. She needs some prompts to help her think of other things to add. She also benefits from a teacher who will write down her details before she forgets.

Serena likes to write. She always thinks of a topic and begins writing right away during writing workshop. Today, Serena asks to publish her piece. I tell her to sign up for a conference.

When we meet, I ask Serena about her picture. She tells me, "It's a picture of recess. Here are Siobhan, Emma, Emelia, and Danika. And this is me."

"What's happening?" I ask.

"We're playing chase," she answers.

"Oh, I see that. Danika must be 'it.' Okay, read me your piece."

Serena reads:

> **My best friend is Emma. We love to play with other friends Siobhan and Emelia. We all love to read books together. We also play outside like we love to run from Danika. Sometimes we have to catch our breath.**

"Okay. You picked a good topic for you, Serena. I like that you tell two things you like to do: read books together and play outside. You also give an example of what you do. You run from Danika. I do have some questions that might help you elaborate a little. Would you mind reading this to me again and I'll stop you when I have a question."

Serena agrees to this. When she gets to the line "We all love to read books together," I stop her and ask her, "What kind of books? Do you like a specific book?"

Serena says, "*Hello Kitty* is one of our favorites. And we like fairy tales."

"Those are great details. You are actually giving examples. Remember, that is a great way to elaborate. May I write your examples right here?"

Serena says, "Yes." I write her details in between the lines.

I ask Serena to continue reading. After she reads, "We love to play outside like we love to run from Danika," I ask Serena to stop again.

"So do you only run from Danika? That doesn't sound like much fun for her."

"Oh no, we chase her too." Then Serena adds, "We get tired."

Again, I ask, "May I add that detail?" I write down Serena's words.

"Okay, let's finish. Read me your last sentence."

Serena reads, "Sometimes we have to catch our breath."

We add a word Serena forgot to write and then I say, "You know, I'm not sure I know your writing is finished. Is there an ending sentence you could write that would sum up your story about your friends and tell your reader you are done writing?"

Serena thinks and says, "Those are my best-friend times."

"That is a wonderful ending sentence and it really does sum up your piece. Could you write that sentence yourself?" (see Figure 7.6). Serena does and our conference is over. We go to the computer to type up her story.

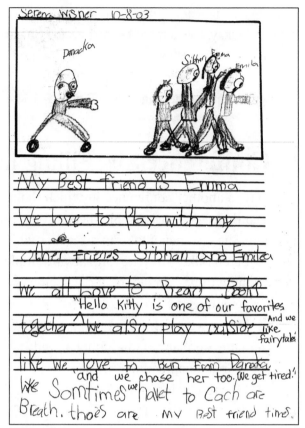

Figure 7.6
Serena's piece with revisions for elaboration.

Conference Seven: Telling "What" and Learning to Slow Down the Moment

Here is an example of a student who can handle some nudging in specific ways to elaborate. He needs my support with part of it, but is able to revise to elaborate on his own for the other part. I nudge him to *tell what* and use a specific technique to slow down the moment.

Johnny is a bright third grader who does not really like to write. He usually sighs when writing workshop starts, often struggling to think of a topic. Today Johnny looks to our ideas chart and decides to write about his pet cat, Suzi.

> **My cat Suzi died 10-10-06. She was forty-two in cat years and six in human years. She was a furry cat and she got shaved 10-6-06. She played a lot.**

I pull up my stool and ask Johnny to read his piece. After he finishes, I ask him to explain his picture at the top. He points to the part of the cat body labeled "where she had cancer," and another part labeled "bullet." He explains, "See, Suzi had cancer and she also was shot with a BB gun."

"Oh. I like your labels. Those are great details you added to your picture. Would you mind reading your piece again to me?"

Johnny reads his story again. I say, "You know, I love your topic. It sounds like Suzi was a special pet. I just feel that I want to know more. Sometimes authors write their stories, but then have more to say. They revise their piece by elaborating." I refer to a mini-lesson I taught earlier that week, in which I modeled revising by adding details to my own story. "Remember earlier this week I wrote about seeing that cat run across the road. When I reread it, I knew my readers would have some unanswered questions. I knew I could add more details to make the story more interesting. So I did." I point out the chart with my writing and revisions, still hanging on the easel.

I come back to Johnny's story. "Right here where you say, 'She played a lot,' I am wondering, '*What* did she play?'"

Johnny answers, "She hid from me and I had to find her."

"Wait," I say. "May I write that down on this sticky note so we don't forget what you said?"

Johnny agrees to this. "Sure."

"Okay. You had to look for her. Remember how questions can help us elaborate? *Where* did you look for her?"

"Johnny answers and I record, "Under a basket or in her spot."

"*Where* is her spot?"

Johnny continues, "Right next to the sticker tree."

Now I tell Johnny, "We can put this sticky note right here and draw an arrow. Then we can draw another arrow where you want to add these ideas. Where would you like to add your details?"

Johnny looks at his piece and points to the part right after "she played a lot." "That's a great place because you're answering the question, 'Where did she play?'"

I continue, "Now, I have one more thing. I notice you ended your piece with 'I had to take care of her.' Do you have anything else you want to say about that? I remember when you read this to me the first time you added something about your mom telling you something about finding her."

Johnny answers, "Oh yeah, she said, 'Since you found her, you have to keep her.'"

"Oh, I love that. If you add that, you will be slowing down the moment by telling what someone said. Remember, authors often elaborate by doing that." I point to one of our charts hanging in the room (see right).

As I leave to work with another student, Johnny is adding his sentence. He asks if he

SLOW DOWN THE MOMENT

✓ tell what you <u>feel</u>

✓ tell what you <u>think</u>

✓ tell what <u>someone said</u>

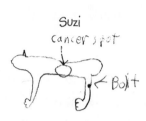

Figure 7.7 shows two boxes. Left box (Johnny's first copy with revisions):

Suzi

[drawing of cat labeled "Were she has cancer", "Bolit"]

my cat suzi DiDe 10-10-06. She was 42 in cat years and 6 in humin years. she was a fury cat and she got shavd 10-6-06. She playd a lot. I had to care for her Because my mom said "sinse you found her you haif to kepp her" and tats what I did.

She hid from me and I had to find her, under a basket or in her spot" right next to sticker tree.

Right box (published piece):

Suzi
cancer spot
[drawing of cat labeled "Bolt"]

My cat Suzi died 10-10-06. She was 42 in cat years and 6 in human years. She was yellow, white, black, and brown. She was a furry cat and she got shaved on 10-6-06.

She played a lot. She hid from me and I had to find her, under a basket or in her spot right next to the sticker tree.

I had to care for her because my mom said, "Since you found her, you have to keep her." and that's what I did.

by Johnny Bartanen
October 12, 2006

Figure 7.7
Johnny's first copy with revisions and his published piece.

can publish his piece. I tell him yes, and he types his piece the next day on our computer in the classroom. Afterward, I edit it for spelling, punctuation, and capitalization. (See Figure 7.7.)

Conference Eight: Tell Me More About That—Telling What and Why

As students progress, I let go and require them to do more of their revisions independently. I still have the conversations that will help them decide what to add, but students are responsible for taking notes and adding the details themselves.

The following student starts with only a few sentences, but because of a one-on-one conversation and a great topic, she is able to independently revise for elaboration.

Richelle comes to me during writing workshop. "I want to read my story so far because I don't know what else to say."

"Okay," I say. I sit down and listen to Richelle read what she has.

> **I love my kitty! Her fur is black and white and orangish-reddish. She is so wonderful to have in the house. She is pretty. Her name is Sassy and sometimes we call her Satan.**

"Wow," I respond. "Let me tell you that I love your description of your cat's color. You are very specific. The part that really piques my interest, though, is the part where you say, 'Her name is Sassy and sometimes we call her Satan.' Oh, my goodness! I have lots of questions. Tell me about why you call your cat Satan. What does she do that made her earn that nickname? I can only imagine!"

Richelle begins to explain that her cat chases her when she runs upstairs, and it is scary because she attacks her. She says, "I also jump on my couch and hide from her when she's under the couch. And her scratches really hurt!"

"Oh, my! Does she do anything else?" I ask.

Richelle answers, "She has a secret hideout under my mom's bed and she takes things from us and hides them there."

"Wow!" You told me a lot more. You really explained why you call your cat Satan. Can you go find a good writing spot and add these details to your writing? It sounds like you have a lot more to add!"

Richelle agrees and works on her piece, revising for details by *telling what* and *why* (see Figure 7.8).

My Kitty

I love my kitty! Her fur is black and white and orangish-reddish. She is so wonderful to have in the house. She is pretty.
Her name is Sassy and sometimes we call her Satan when she is wild. When I run upstairs, Sassy runs after me. It is scary. When Sassy is under the couch we run up on the couch and hide. Sassy jumps up and finds us and attacks us.
When Sassy scratches it hurts! When we run by the couch she runs after you and attacks you and it hurts.
When I'm bored, I go into my mom's bedroom and run up on the bed. Sassy jumps up and attacks me. Under my mom's bed Sassy has a secret hideout. She takes stuff from us and takes them to her hideout. I just love my kitty!

Figure 7.8
Richelle's revised writing.

Conference Nine: Using Description as a Way of Elaborating

I love publishing conferences because sometimes the best revision comes when we begin typing. Such is the case with Serena. We have only one computer in the room, so because of that, and the age of my students, I do a lot of the typing of stories, poems, and nonfiction. I rarely type after school (unless I have had a thorough conference). Instead, students sit by my side as I type, and in doing so, have another opportunity to revise or edit, as well as decide all of the practical things about publishing: which way the paper will face, where the text should go (at the top or bottom of the page), which font seems to fit their piece.

Serena had written a piece titled "My Senses at the Pond." She wrote a considerable amount and was ready to publish. We sit down at the computer and Serena reads as I type, "One fine day I was walking along to the pond. I had my yellow raincoat on me. I saw a turtle waddling slowly to the pond too. Then the clouds began to spill rain."

At this point I began to get ahead, typing the next word of the following sentence. "Wait!" Serena says. "I want to add something. '. . . rain that was dropping like leaves falling gently to the ground.'"

I back up and say, "Oh. That is beautiful. You used a simile to describe the rain."

Serena smiles because she knows she is applying something she learned in a recent mini-lesson: using language as a way to slow down the moment.

Serena continues reading and I continue typing.

While I was there I heard birds chirping their sweet song.

My Senses at the Pond
By Serena Wisner
April, 2003

One fine spring day I was walking along to the pond. I had my yellow raincoat on and saw a turtle waddling slowly to the pond too. Then the clouds began to spill rain, rain that was dropping like leaves falling gently to the ground.

While I was there I heard birds chirping their sweet song, singing, *chirp, chirp, chirp, chirp,* frogs croaking, the rain dripping to the ground, falling in the puddles, making the noise, *splash splash.* I saw cattails waving in the wind. I felt the wind rubbing against my cheeks. The crickets went *crick, crick* and I heard the mud squishing on my boots as I walked in it. I smelled the moisture, the smell so sweet, the pond so fresh, the mud smelling like wet dirt, and I feel so happy that I want to jump up and splash in the puddles!

The rain hits my nose. I feel wet from the rain, tired from today's walk. I feel the cattails rubbing at my cheeks as I finally run home to tell my mom that a fun time I had and to have some delicious hot cocoa.

Figure 7.9
Serena's published piece "My Senses at the Pond."

Serena turns to me and says, "I should say what their sweet song is."
"Okay. Tell me what to type."

. . . singing chirp, chirp, chirp.

When she gets to the part about the noise the rain made in the mud, she adds, "splash, splash."

In the course of reading her piece, Serena adds things she sensed that were not in her original piece. After "I smelled the moisture," she adds: "the smell so sweet, the pond so fresh, the mud smelling like wet dirt. . ."

After "I feel wet from the rain," she adds: ". . .tired from today's walk."

When I finish typing, Serena rereads her piece to make sure it says everything she wants it to. I tell her, "You know, when I sit down to type what I have written, I often make changes too. Good authors are always revising to make their writing better. You did that today. You added interesting language and extended ideas and sentences. You described in more detail. I am proud of you!" (See Figure 7.9.)

Final Thoughts

One-on-one conferences are an important element of every good writing program. Students need to have undivided attention, a time when the teacher is focused solely on them and their work. This is the place students can be encouraged, nudged, celebrated, and even pushed to do better work.

When I teach a series of mini-lessons on elaborating, the conference is a time when I see whether students are applying what's been taught. I prod students to try one new thing, such as adding a word, or elaborating by giving examples or definitions, or even by giving a statistic or fact. I tell students when something is unclear because there is not enough information and encourage them to add more details. The conference is a time when I help students consider new topics and gather ideas in a way that will help them with their writing. Conferences for me are just one-on-one mini-lessons. I can't imagine teaching writing effectively without them.

ASSESSMENT AND ELABORATION: GATHERING DATA AND DOCUMENTING GROWTH

Assessment has gotten a bad rap in recent years. We associate it with No Child Left Behind, as well as with state tests requiring students to meet a set standard to graduate from high school, or sometimes to pass on to the next grade level. Some of these punitive assessments make no sense to me. When we simply ask ourselves if a student "made it," we are evaluating, not assessing. Ideally, good assessment should enable a teacher to diagnose students' needs and inform teachers' instructional decisions in addition to allowing teachers to see whether each child has "got it."

While I have serious problems with NCLB, I do believe in accountability. Teachers (and I am one) should be accountable for teaching students what they need to know and making sure that they are learning these skills and concepts.

When I began teaching, over twenty years ago, we had Student Learning Objectives or SLOs. These were lists of objectives to be taught by the teacher. Every grade level had a list for each subject. When we taught the objective, we checked it off. It didn't matter whether students learned, as long as we taught what was on the list.

As our state moved to reform in the early 1990s, a relevant cartoon circulated through assessment workshops. It showed a dog and two children. The cartoon had three frames. The first frame showed one child telling the other child that he had taught his dog to whistle. Frame two showed the dog just sitting there. In the third frame the first child says, "I said I taught him. I didn't say he learned it."

Now instead of SLOs we have GLEs (Grade Level Expectations). The key word here is "expectations." What are students expected to know and be able to do by the end of first, second, third, or fourth grade? This is the question we ask. This is our focus as we plan, teach, and assess students in our classroom.

Our GLEs for writing are clear. As far as elaborating on ideas, kindergarten students are to use words and pictures to express ideas. They may dictate ideas that match pictures and can tell stories orally. First graders are to write about a chosen idea, and add simple sentences to elaborate on those ideas. By second grade students should be able to write with more flow, maintain focus, and be able to elaborate on ideas with description and examples. And by the time students finish third and fourth grades, they should be able to write a couple to several paragraphs, elaborating on ideas using various techniques. They should be able to develop characters and settings in a written story, as well as provide supportive information. They also should use personal experience and observation to support ideas.

Of course our GLEs also include writing with a sense of organization, fluency, voice, and word choice, as well as using age-appropriate conventions. I have zeroed in on choosing topics and elaborating on ideas because these are the areas young students need to experiment with first. They need to learn to choose topics that are meaningful and they need to write with detail about those topics.

Three Student Portfolios

Portfolios of student writing are invaluable as teachers document growth. Samples of student writing collected over the year can be one's best indicator of the kind of growth a student makes. The key is not to collect so many pieces that they get lost in one big bundle of paper. In first grade, more samples are needed at the beginning of the year, because students change in skill level so quickly. As the year progresses, and in second, third, and fourth grades, one might collect six to eight samples during the year. This will give teachers enough work to really see what a child can do and how she has grown.

Let's take a look at three students and their growth in the area of elaboration. Obviously there will be growth in other areas as well: writing with purpose and a sense of voice, using interesting language, writing fluent sentences, including leads and endings, as well as using appropriate conventions. I believe we should look at a student's whole piece of writing. As I comment, I will address the entire student work, but will focus mostly on growth in elaborating on ideas.

ROBBIE

Robbie is a student who came to first grade without much experience in writing. His first few pieces were drawings in which he dictated his stories: "School is fun." "I like going hunting with my dad." Even this second piece shows improvement in the area of elaboration. Robbie tells us what he likes to do (hunting) and then tells who he goes hunting with (his dad). Robbie's drawings show more detail with each piece. At first he uses one color and then as the days go by, he begins to use several colors in his drawings. Robbie also adds more to his pictures with each piece. His paper becomes crowded with figures: people, trees, animals, buildings, and so on.

Now Robbie is ready to write his message himself. We read *Oliver Button* by Tomie dePaola. Robbie responds to this book with the following: "I feel bad" (see Figure 8.1).

It is clear that Robbie is still learning sound-symbol correspondence. He includes some matching letters (*F* and *L*). However, the important thing is that Robbie has an idea. He chose not to add a detail, probably because this was his first attempt to write his message himself. He includes a picture that has three people, and one might infer that there may be some sort of elaboration to his story there.

A couple of months later, Robbie chooses to write a book titled *My Fish* (see Figure 8.2). His cover shows some detail with a couple of fish, along with a jellyfish. On Robbie's first page he writes, "I got a fish." His drawing is small and simple. His second page reads "I change the fish's water." Here Robbie's picture shows more detail. Page three is wordless, but the picture shows a happy fish with bubbles. On his last page Robbie writes, "I feed my fish." Again, Robbie shows a smile on the fish in the tank.

Robbie came up with his own topic. He told his reader that he got a fish and then added two details about how he takes care of his fish.

In early spring of first grade, Robbie writes about the lake by his house.

Figure 8.1
Robbie writes "I feel bad."

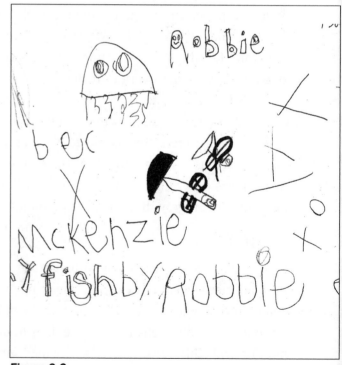

Figure 8.2
Robbie's book titled "My Fish."

> I have a lake by my house. I go kayaking and canoeing and I
> go fishing and I go scuba diving and I jump off a high rock into
> the lake. Lakes are water with land all around.

It is clear Robbie has an idea and he has lots of details to share. They come out in a list-like fashion, and my next step might be to have him stop at each activity and tell more about it. For instance, after he writes "I go kayaking and canoeing," I could prod him to tell me what he does during those activities and who he does them with. After "I jump off a high rock," I could ask, "How does that feel when you jump off that high rock and land in the water? Tell me more about that."

Robbie makes his biggest impression on me with his last sentence: "Lakes are water with land all around." We had been studying landforms and we also had been learning about using definitions to elaborate on ideas. Robbie takes what he learns in both social studies and writing, and applies them here. He elaborates with the definition of a lake.

Fast-forward six months to October of second grade. Robbie writes about his favorite season.

> One of my favorite seasons is winter because there is snow
> and I get to see my cousins and I get to open presents and this
> year I am going to try to wake up when Santa Claus comes. I
> love sledding in the snow. I love having snowball fights and hot
> cocoa by the fire.

Robbie tells us that winter is one of his favorite seasons and then gives some reasons why. It begins as somewhat of a list, but then he adds: "This year I am going to try to wake up when Santa comes." That is a great little anecdote. He goes on to add some other relevant details about what he loves to do in winter ("I love sliding in the snow. I love having snowball fights") and then he adds a beautiful detail to end his piece ("and hot cocoa by the fire").

Again, in a one-on-one conference I would prod Robbie to elaborate about a few of the things he mentions: telling how, why, who, what, or when. However, when I look at Robbie's writing from a year ago and compare this piece to that, as well as the other first-grade pieces, clearly, Robbie shows growth in his ability to elaborate.

JARRED

Jarred is a third grader. He comes from a second-grade classroom with a wonderful teacher who favors a writing workshop style. Jarred is used to choosing topics, but he still has a difficult time some days. Often I hear, "I don't know what to write about." In September Jarred writes: "On summer vacation I went to Canada with my dad to see one of his friends."

After a short conference with Jarred, in which I try to get him to elaborate, he adds, "It was a long flight" (see Figure 8.3).

October, November, and December do not bring much gain in the area of elaboration for Jarred. In October he writes, "My favorite season is October because I like carving jack-o-lanterns and trick-or-treating. October is a fun season" (see Figure 8.4).

He writes a lead sentence, adds two sparse details about what he likes to do, and then includes an ending sentence.

In November Jarred writes, "I only like rain when it makes rainbows and lightning and thunder. I hate rain because it gets you soaking wet and makes mud (see Figure 8.5).

Here Jarred takes two sides and gives reasons for both, so there is a little improvement in elaborating on ideas, but still he is just listing a few details.

Fast-forward a few months. All year up to this point, I have been teaching lessons on elaborating on ideas. Students learn about using their senses to describe, giving examples and anecdotes, and telling who, why, when, where, and what as ways to tell more.

Figure 8.3
Jarred writes about summer vacation.

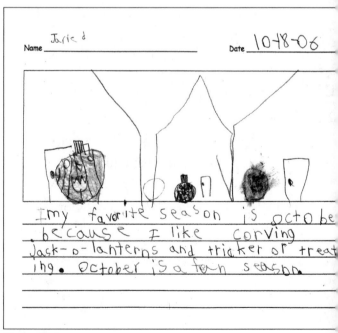

Figure 8.4
Jarred writes about a favorite time of year.

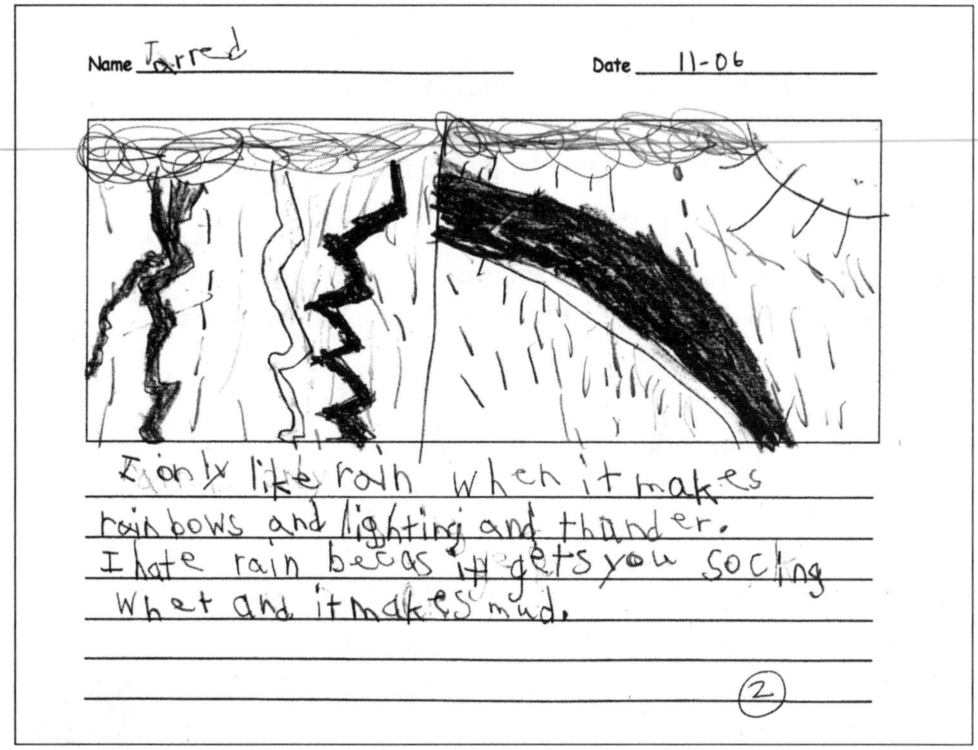

Name Jarred   **Date** 11-06

I only like rain when it makes rainbows and lighting and thander. I hate rain becas it gets you soaking whet and it makes mud.

②

Figure 8.5
Jarred writes about the rain.

I model writing. Students participate in shared writing. I hold conferences to help students revise for elaborating on ideas.

In March Jarred writes to a prompt. He tells about his favorite place.

> **My favorite place is at school during choice time. I like choice time because I love to do stuff with dominoes. I love to watch the dominoes fall really fast. Faster and faster they go. The bigger the domino creation, the faster they go. My favorite thing to do with dominoes is make cool stuff like walls, battling rams, escalators, stars, and last but not least towers. I love dominoes.**

Jarred has undoubtedly improved in his writing in more ways than one. He tells what his favorite place is, and then he tells why.

> **I like choice time because I love to do stuff with dominos.**

Jarred goes on to tell what he does with the dominos and adds a very nice sentence to describe in more detail.

> **I love to watch the dominos fall really fast. Faster and faster they go.**

Then Jarred explains an observation he has made.

The bigger the domino creation, the faster they go.

Now Jarred turns his attention to telling what he likes to do with dominos and here he elaborates with examples using the word *like*.

My favorite thing to do with dominoes is make cool stuff like walls, battling rams, escalators, stars, and last but not least, towers.

Jarred ends his piece to let his reader know he is finished.

I love dominoes.

It is clear that Jarred is finally applying what he has learned in order to stay focused and elaborate on his ideas. He tells what, explains why, and gives examples to tell more about his favorite activity at school.

Jarred's last sample comes in June. Here we find out what Jarred really has learned as a writer, including elaborating on ideas. Jarred writes:

I like summer because there is a gentle breeze and I like to fill up my pool and float my rain gutter boat. First I check the wind. It's hard to explain how to set the sail; you just have to experiment. When the wind blows and the sail is set right, it should race forwards or tip over onto its side.

One time I somehow made it go out and race forward after turning back to me and another time it went out and turned a bit and went fast forward and the shape of the path it took was the shape of a piece of pie. I love summer.

Jarred clearly has learned to express himself in writing. Not only does he elaborate by telling why he loves summer, he gives specific examples, painting a picture for us, making us feel like we're there. Jarred includes two anecdotes ("One time . . ." and "another time") to tell about specific moments. He tells about the "gentle breeze" and what happens when the "wind blows." Jarred takes us to his time in summer and describes for us what it is like.

LINNAE

Linnae is a second grader with a talent for writing. She has her own voice and style. She considers her audience and has many stories to tell. Linnae comes to second grade already strong in elaborating on ideas.

Linnae's first piece is a book titled "My Pet Had Babies."

> **One day my cat was gone! We looked everywhere but we couldn't find her. Where could she be?**
>
> **We looked outside. We looked in the forest. We couldn't find her. She was gone for two weeks. We looked everywhere outside but we couldn't find her. Where could she have gone?**
>
> **Then I went home, looked some more. I found her! She was behind the TV. She was having babies! She had ten babies. That's a lot.**

Linnae's voice shines through in her writing. She elaborates by telling what she is thinking: "Where could she be?" "Where could she have gone?" and by telling where they looked: "We looked outside. We looked in the forest. We looked everywhere. . ." Linnae also tells where she found her. "She was behind the TV."

Linnae's second piece comes later that fall. This one is about snakes.

> **Snakes don't blink. Snakes eat rats. It wraps its long body around the rat. Then the snake starts to squeeze. Tight . . . tighter . . . tighter. Soon the rat's heart stops. Then the snake eats it. Many snakes use poison to kill their food. Snakes eat smaller snakes. Snakes live in woods. They don't live where it is cold.**

Linnae writes very well for a second grader at this time of year. She gives lots of details about snakes: where they live, what they eat, and how they catch their prey. She definitely elaborates but does so in a somewhat unorganized way. She begins with a random fact: Snakes don't blink. Then her best sentences come, when she tells about snakes eating rats. She describes the process. At the end of her piece she tells where snakes live. Still, for a second grader at this time of year, I consider Linnae a solid writer, doing a good job elaborating on ideas.

In February, Linnae writes a book about dolphins. This time she follows a format we used in a shared writing piece about pandas (see Chapter 3). As Linnae writes about her animal, it is clear that she is applying learned strategies for elaborating. On her first page alone, she tells more by giving a definition, telling what dolphins do and how they do it, and using some descriptive language.

"WHAT IS A DOLPHIN?"

A dolphin is a mammal. That is an animal that doesn't lay eggs and it means they feed on milk. Dolphins have blow holes. They use their blow holes for breathing. What they do is they jump out of the water and into the air. Then they squirt water out of the blow hole. They are very slippery creatures.

On page two Linnae writes about what dolphins eat.

"WHAT DO DOLPHINS EAT?"

Dolphins eat fish called krill, anchovies, and lots more. When dolphins find a school of fish they call the pod over and they all take turns swallowing the delicious fish. To a dolphin it's tasty. To us it's gross.

Here, Linnae elaborates by telling what dolphins eat, giving us examples. She also tells how dolphins hunt the fish, taking turns. At the end of the page Linnae adds her own comment as a way of elaborating and projecting voice into the piece.

Linnae's book continues exploring how dolphins move, where dolphins live, the different kinds of dolphins there are, what dolphins like to do, and how dolphins protect themselves. On each page Linnae elaborates by giving definitions and examples, telling where, and adding interesting personal comments. She is clearly applying elaboration strategies learned during mini-lessons. This shines brightly in her work.

Yes, Linnae came to second grade with strong writing skills. She loves to write and would probably have picked up a lot on her own, because she is motivated and passionate about writing. However, it is clear that intentional teaching can make a difference with our best writers too.

Figure 8.6
The cover of Linnae's dolphin book.

Writing Prompts

I am a big proponent of students choosing their own topics. Mem Fox lists "choice of topic" as the first consideration for writing or teaching writing (1993). When students choose their topics, their writing is more specific. They have a voice, and that voice shines through in their words. Almost always, I am more impressed with writing in which the topic has been chosen by the student, as opposed to being chosen by me.

However, there are times students must write to a particular topic. This happens for state reading and writing tests and possible performance assessments in the classroom. If I fail to give students practice with writing to a teacher-chosen topic, I am doing them a disservice.

Therefore, I have learned to write the best prompts I can. I work with colleagues to consider topics that students are interested in, and have some background knowledge about. In Chapter 2 I speak about the best topics being ones we 1) know about, and 2) like or are interested in. I don't want to write a prompt that contradicts this belief.

So, what makes a good writing prompt? I am certainly not an expert, but I know some rules to follow. One accepted rule is TAP. Every good prompt includes a topic (T), an audience (A), and a purpose (P). The topic is *what* I will write about; the audience is *who* I am writing for; and the purpose is *why* I am writing this (to tell, to explain, to persuade, to inform). Sometimes a prompt might include format (F), as well. Format is *how* I will present my writing (book, paper, letter, journal entry).

Here is an example of a prompt that includes TAP.

> Pick an animal you find fascinating and explain to your classmates why you find this animal so fascinating.

In this prompt, animal is the *topic,* classmates are the *audience*, and the *purpose* is to explain.

Here is a another prompt:

> You are walking through the woods. Suddenly you look down and there is a box. You open it up. Tell what you find in the box.

This prompt includes a *topic* (what's inside the box). It also include a *purpose* (to tell*)*, but it is missing an *audience*. Who is the writer telling? Often, state tests will assume the writer knows the audience is the test scorers and so they will not always include an audience in the prompt.

Here is a third prompt:

> Tell a friend about a special time you had with your family.

The *topic* is a special time. The *audience* is a friend. The *purpose* is to tell.

Now you try identifying whether these are well-written prompts. Is there a topic, audience, and purpose?

Imagine you are traveling on the Oregon Trail. Explain to a relative back home about the hardships on your journey.

Write about your favorite place.

The principal is considering stopping popcorn sales during Tuesday recess. Write a letter to him explaining why popcorn sales should continue.

You want to play baseball during recess. Write a letter to your principal.

Tell a friend what you like about the rain and what you don't like about the rain. Explain why.

SCORING PAPERS

I give writing prompts several times each year to see how students will write to a topic they have not chosen. I try to pick topics that are relevant and interesting. I often score these pieces holistically, looking at elaboration, leads and endings, use of language, voice, and sentence fluency. I consider what I have taught thus far and the grade level of the child, and then I set my expectations. I also score papers for conventions. Again, I set the standard based on what I think students should be able to do at that time of year.

I am careful with rubrics. They are useful when talking with staff about students' writing. However, it is important when we assign numbers to papers, that we understand what those numbers mean. We need to be in agreement about what a 3 (meeting the standard) means. We need to define it for students and for teachers scoring and discussing student work. While teaching a multi-age classroom, I may give the same writing prompt, but my standard for second graders will be different from my standard for third graders. A score of 3 for a second grader might be a 2 for a third grader.

ANECDOTAL NOTES

I also think rubrics are overused. I am much happier describing student work anecdotally. Yes, a score can be helpful, but students (and I) don't need a score for every piece of writing. Sometimes feedback comes in the form of written praise and a challenge on a sticky note for the student (see Figure 8.7).

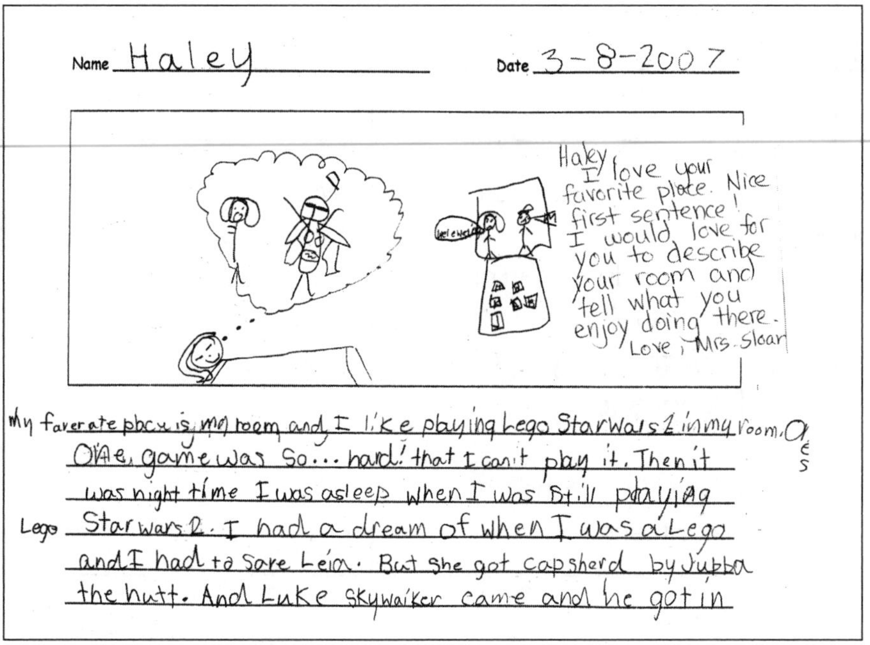

Figure 8.7
Comments to Haley about her writing.

RECORD KEEPING: ANECDOTAL NOTES Sometimes I make notes on a sheet (see page 137) or in my assessment notebook during writing conferences. Each child has a section. I write about my observations, their strengths, and next steps for teaching.

OBSERVATIONS	STRENGTHS	NEXT STEPS

Miya writes about her favorite place:

One of my favorite places is the public library. I like going in the adult section. I also like going in the kid section. My favorite thing to do is pick a good book and sit on the couch and read. One time where I was reading a fantastic book and my dad was on the search. He couldn't find his book and said it was time to find my books, but I couldn't hear him. I was attached to the story. I usually get four horse books. I love the library.

Here are my notes:

OBSERVATIONS	STRENGTHS	NEXT STEPS
*Favorite place—library Has a passion for her subject, wrote one paragraph, has the start of a second paragraph.	Includes anecdote "I couldn't hear him because I was attached to the story."—Great language. Nice word choice (fantastic)	Work on a second paragraph focused on horse books? Spell-check card for "like"

Figure 8.8
My anecdotal notes about Miya's piece.

These notes are helpful to me as I assess Miya's growth in areas such as elaboration, as well as plan future mini-lessons.

RECORD KEEPING: SCORING PAPERS AND ANECDOTAL NOTES

Sometimes, to see the growth students are making, I record scores for papers, as well as write anecdotal notes (see page 138). I take a class list and make a column for each prompt topic. There are two scores in each box next to the student names. The first score is for content (ideas, organization, and style). The second score is a conventions score. After reading papers, I score them and then I write a quick note if something sticks out to me.

After reading all of the papers, I look for trends. Figure 8.9 shows all of the places I wrote "needs details" or "lacks details." Not only was this great information in assessing students on elaboration, but it helped me

A teacher-student conference.

Wtg · Prompts

Mrs. Sloan's Class 2006-2007

Student Names	Animal 11/06		Rain 11/06	
1. Lily	2 / 2		2 / 2	
2. Stephen	2 / 3	needs details	2 / 3	needs details
3. Ellissa	1			
4. Hannah	3+/4 / 3+		2+/3	needs details
5. Tim	2+/3 / 2+	needs caps good spelling	2 / 3+	needs details
6. Jess	1/(2) / 3	details need	2 / 3	needs details but good lang.
7. Sean	2/(3) / 3	needs caps	3 / 3	needs details good w.c.
8. Kayla				
9. Rebecca	2/3 / 3	needs details	3 / 3	
10. Zack	3 / 2+		3+ / 3	need caps/periods
11. Josh	3+ / 3		2+/3 / 2	
12. Brianna	3 / 3		3 / 3	anecdote
13. Caity	4 / 4		3 / 4	
14. Adam	3/4 / 4		4 / 4	
15. Emily	4 / 3+		4 / 3	
16. Cristen	2/(3) / 3	needs details	2+/3 / 3	
17. Collin	2/(3) / 2+		2 / 3	lacks details needs caps
18. Devin	3 / 2		3 / 2	nice stories
19. Andrea	4 / 3+		4 / 4	
20. Jamison	3 / 4		3 / 3	word choice -cap
21. Brooks	1 / 2	needs details	1 / 1	
22.				
23.				

↑ Conventions   ↑ Conventions

Figure 8.9
Student scores and anecdotal notes on class list.

plan my next mini-lessons. It was clear that I needed to model, and have students participate in shared writing lessons focused on adding details. I needed to read books, pointing out how authors elaborate in different ways. I chose to do some of these lessons with the whole class, but I also pulled those seven or eight children who were struggling with how to elaborate in their writing and taught some small-group lessons on adding details.

Good assessment gives valid information about students, and also informs instruction. If a number does not tell me enough, I need to also write anecdotal notes. These can be short and to the point. I also need to consider students. I can tell them information that will celebrate and guide their work. I can also write notes to them to help them recognize their strengths and also the areas they need to work on.

Final Thoughts

The goals of classroom writing assessment are to document growth, communicate that growth to students and parents, and inform instruction. When I consider my assessments, I must consider my goals. I want to document growth, so I have students:

- keep a portfolio with writing samples
- take periodic writing performance assessments (writing to a prompt)
- observe students and record anecdotal notes about the writing process
- record anecdotal notes and scores of papers

I also want to communicate that growth to students and parents, so I:

- hold writing conferences with students, discuss their progress, and guide them to be better writers

- share my notes and scores with students and parents

Assessment should also inform instruction, so I notice and mark trends I see such as:

- students need help elaborating on ideas
- students need help with where to end one sentence and begin a new one
- students need help with closing lines or paragraphs to let their reader know their work is finished
- students need help using interesting language

Consider a classroom without assessment. A teacher would have to guess how students grow and perform. That's not good enough. It is important that we know how students grow and perform. We need to know so that we can report this information to students and parents. We need to know so that we can plan our next lessons. And we need to know so that we know we are teaching what we should be teaching, and when and how we should be teaching it.

APPENDIX

Name _____

Learning to Elaborate

Original Sentence	Elaboration
Original Sentence	Elaboration
Original Sentence	Elaboration
Original Sentence	Elaboration
Original Sentence	Elaboration
Original Sentence	Elaboration

Name _____

Animal Research

My animal is a _____

Looks like

_____

_____

Sounds it makes:

_____

_____

_____

Where it lives:

_____

_____

_____

How it moves:

_____

_____

_____

What it eats:

_____

_____

_____

Other interesting facts:

_____

_____

_____

_____

Interesting words I could use in describing my animal:

_____

_____

Name _____

Animal Research

My animal: _____

What is a _____ ? Looks: Sounds:	Where do _____ live?
What do _____ eat?	How do _____ move?
Other interesting facts:	Other interesting facts:

Anecdotal Notes

Name _____

Date	Observations	Strengths	Next Steps

Class Scores and Anecdotal Notes

Name	Scores	Notes	Scores	Notes
1.				
2.				
3.				
4.				
5.				
6.				
7.				
8.				
9.				
10.				
11.				
12.				
13.				
14.				
15.				
16.				
17.				
18.				
19.				
20.				
21.				
22.				
23.				
24.				
25.				

Children's Books

Abercrombie, B. (1990). *Charlie Anderson.* New York: Aladdin.

Adler, D. (1980). *Cam Jansen: The mystery of the stolen diamonds.* New York: Puffin.

Adler, D. (1983). *Our amazing ocean.* Mahwah, NJ: Troll Associates.

Adler, D. (1990). *A picture book of Helen Keller.* New York: The Trumpet Club.

Adler, D. (1992). *A picture book of Harriet Tubman.* New York: Scholastic.

Adler, D. (1993). *A picture book of Rosa Parks.* New York: Scholastic.

Allen, J., & Humphries, T. (2002). *Are you a grasshopper?* Boston: Kingfisher.

Arnold, C. (1993). *Prairie dogs.* New York: Scholastic.

Arnosky, J. (1998). *All about turkeys.* New York: Scholastic.

Avi. (1990). *The true confessions of Charlotte Doyle.* New York: HarperTrophy.

Avi. (1995). *Poppy.* New York: HarperTrophy.

Avi. (2000). *Ereth's birthday.* New York: HarperTrophy.

Avi. (2002) *Crispin: The cross of lead.* New York: Hyperion.

Berger, M. (1995). *A whale is not a fish and other animal mix-ups.* New York: Scholastic.

Berger, M. & G. (2001). *Does it always rain in the rainforest? Questions and answers about tropical rainforests.* New York: Scholastic.

Berger, M. & G. (2003). *Spinning spiders.* China: HarperCollins.

Brenner, M. (1994). *Abe Lincoln's hat.* New York: Scholastic.

Brown, J. (1964). *Flat Stanley.* New York: HarperCollins.

Byles, M. (1990). *Life in the polar lands.* New York: Scholastic.

Caisley, R. (1994). *Raewyn's got the writing bug again.* Singapore: SRA.

Cannon, J. (1993). *Stellaluna.* San Diego: Harcourt Brace.

Caudill, R. (1966). *Did you carry the flag today, Charley?* New York: Dell Publishing.

Cleary, B. (1975). *Ramona the brave.* New York: HarperCollins.

Cooney, B. (1982). *Miss Rumphius.* New York: Viking.

Dahl, R. (1961). *James and the giant peach.* New York: Knopf.

Dahl, R. (1964). *Charlie and the chocolate factory.* New York: Knopf.

Danziger, P. (1999). *I, Amber Brown.* New York: Putnam.

DeCesare, A. (1999). *Flip's fantastic journal.* New York: Dutton.

DePaola, T. (1979). *Oliver Button is a sissy.* New York: Voyager.

Dewin, H. (2006). *The dog: Why are dogs' noses wet? and other true facts.* New York: Scholastic.

DiCamillo, K. (2000). *Because of Winn-Dixie.* Cambridge, MA: Candlewick Press.

DiCamillo, K. (2003). *The tale of Despereaux.* Cambridge, MA: Candlewick Press.

Edwards, P. (1999). *Barefoot: Escape on the underground railroad.* New York: HarperCollins.

Fleming, D. (1993). *In the small, small pond.* New York: Henry Holt.

Fowler, A. (1992). *Frogs and toads and tadpoles too.* New York: Scholastic.

Fowler, A. (1992). *Turtles take their time.* New York: Scholastic.

Gaff, J. (2002). *I wonder why the Sahara is cold at night: and other questions about deserts.* Boston: Kingfisher.

Gibbons, G. (1996). *Deserts.* New York: Holiday House.

Gibbons, G. (2006). *Owls.* New York: Holiday House.

Greenway, S. (1992). *Animals Q & A: Can you see me?* Nashville: Ideals Publishing Corporation.

Greenway, S. (1992). *Animals Q & A: Whose baby am I?* Nashville: Ideals Publishing Corporation.

Hannigan, K. (2004). *Ida B.* New York: Greenwillow.

Hibbert, A. (1999). *A freshwater pond.* New York: Crabtree Publishing.

Hirschmann, K. (2004). *Rocks and minerals.* New York: Scholastic.

Howe, J. (2002). *It came from beneath the bed.* New York: Atheneum.

Jefferies, L. (1983). *All about stars.* Mahwah, NJ: Troll Associates.

Johnston, T., & dePaola, T. (1985). *The quilt story.* New York: Putnam.

Jordan, A. (2007). *The cat: Why do cats purr? And other true facts.* New York: Scholastic.

Kamm, A. (2002). *If you lived with the Indians of the Northwest Coast.* New York: Scholastic.

Kamm, A. (2004). *If you lived when there was slavery in America.* New York: Scholastic.

Krensky, S. (2004). *Davy Crockett: A life on the frontier.* New York: Simon & Schuster.

Krensky, S. (2001). *Egypt.* New York: Scholastic.

Krull, K. (2003). *Harvesting hope: The story of Cesar Chavez.* New York: Harcourt.

Levenson, G. (1999). *Pumpkin circle: The story of a garden.* Berkeley: Tricycle Press.

Lithgow, J., & Kenah, K. (2005). *A crash, a roar, and so much more!* Columbus, OH: School Specialty Publishing.

London, J. (1993). *The eyes of Gray Wolf.* San Francisco: Chronicle.

London, J. (1996). *Red wolf country.* New York: Dutton.

London, J. (1999). *Baby whale's journey.* New York: Scholastic.

MacLachlan, P. (1994). *All the places to love.* New York: HarperCollins.

Martin, B. Jr. (1967). *Brown bear, brown bear, what do you see?* New York: Henry Holt.

McGovern, A. (1973). *The Pilgrims' first Thanksgiving.* New York: Scholastic.

McGovern, A. (1995). *Questions and answers about sharks.* New York: Scholastic.

Nelson, S., & Nelson, T. (1997). *Olympic National Park.* New York: Children's Press.

Nicholas, C. (1999). *Know-it-alls: Spiders!* New York: McClanahan Book Company, Inc.

Nicholas, C. (1999). *Know-it-alls: Wolves!* New York: McClanahan Book Company, Inc.

Nicholas, C. (2000). *Know-it-alls: Lizards!* New York: McClanahan Book Company, Inc.

Nichols, C. (2002). *Harriet Tubman.* New York: Scholastic.

O'Brien, R. C. (1971). *Mrs. Frisby and the rats of NIMH.* New York: Aladdin.

Osborne, M. P. (2000). *Civil War on Sunday.* New York: Random House.

Osborne, M. P. (2002). *Good morning, gorillas.* New York: Random House.

Otto, C. B. (2000). *Wolves.* New York: Scholastic.

Park, F., & Park, G. (2000). *The royal bee.* Honesdale, PA: Boyds Mills.

Polacco, P. (1995). *My ol' man.* New York: Philomel Books.

Polacco, P. (1998). *Thank you, Mr. Falker.* New York: Philomel Books.

Polacco, P. (2001). *Mr. Lincoln's way.* New York: Philomel.

Prap, L. (2005). *Why?* La Jolla, CA: Kane/Miller.

Radunsky, V. (2004). *What does peace feel like?* New York: Atheneum.

Rockwell, T. (1973). *How to eat fried worms.* New York: Yearling.

Rockwell, J. (1984). *All about ponds.* Mahwah, NJ: Troll Associates.

Rudy, L. J. (2005). *Snakes!* New York: HarperCollins.

Scrace, C. (1999). *The journey of a turtle.* New York: Franklin Watts.

Schofield, J. (2004). *Animal babies in ponds and rivers.* Boston: Kingfisher.

Schofield, J. (2004). *Animal babies in rain forests.* Boston: Kingfisher.

Shannon, D. (1994). *How Georgie Radbourne saved baseball.* New York: Scholastic.

Spinelli, E. (2001). *Sophie's masterpiece.* New York: Simon & Schuster.

Staples, S. F. (2003). *The green dog.* New York: Farrar, Straus.

Steig, W. (1986). *Brave Irene.* New York: Farrar, Straus.

Sutcliffe, J. (2002). *Paul Revere.* Minneapolis: Lerner Publications.

Venezia, M. (1990). *Monet.* Chicago: Children's Press.

Vogt, G. (2001). *Solar system.* New York: Scholastic.

Walsh, M. (2000). *Do donkeys dance?* London: Egmont Books.

Wiles, D. (2001). *Love, Ruby Lavender.* Orlando: Harcourt.

Wiles, D. (2005). *Each little bird that sings.* Orlando: Harcourt.

White, E. B. (1952). *Charlotte's web.* New York: Harper.

White, E. B. (1970). *The trumpet of the swan.* New York: Scholastic.

Williams, S. (1997). *I went walking.* New York: MacMillan/McGraw-Hill.

Wong, J. (2002). *You have to write.* New York: Margaret K. McElderry.

Yolen, J. (1987). *Owl moon.* New York: Philomel.

Zolotow, C. (1992). *The seashore book.* New York: HarperCollins.

Professional Books

Calkins, L., Hartman, A., & White, Z. (2005). *One to one.* Portsmouth, NH: Heinemann.

Culham, R. (2003). *6 + 1 traits of writing: The complete guide, grades 3 and up.* New York: Scholastic.

Fletcher, R. (1993). *What a writer needs.* Portsmouth, NH: Heinemann.

Flynn, N., & McPhillips, S. (2000) *A note slipped under the door: Teaching from poems we love.* Portland, ME: Stenhouse.

Fox, M. (1993). *Radical reflections.* San Diego: Harcourt Brace.

Graves, D. (1994). *A fresh look at writing.* Portsmouth, NH: Heinemann.

Routman, R. (2005). *Writing essentials.* Portsmouth, NH: Heinemann.

Stiggins, R,. & Spandel, V. (1997). *Creating writers.* Boston: Addison Wesley.

NOTES